REVISE EDEXCEL GCSE (9–1)
History
CRIME AND PUNISHMENT IN BRITAIN, c1000–present

D1460982

REVISION
GUIDE AND WORKBOOK

Series Consultant: Harry Smith

Author: Kirsty Taylor

A note from the publisher

In order to ensure that this resource offers high-quality support for the associated Pearson qualification, it has been through a review process by the awarding body. This process confirms that this resource fully covers the teaching and learning content of the specification or part of a specification at which it is aimed. It also confirms that it demonstrates an appropriate balance between the development of subject skills, knowledge and understanding, in addition to preparation for assessment.

Endorsement does not cover any guidance on assessment activities or processes (e.g. practice questions or advice on how to answer assessment questions) included in the resource, nor does it prescribe any particular approach to the teaching or delivery of a related course.

While the publishers have made every attempt to ensure that advice on the qualification and its assessment is accurate, the official specification and associated assessment guidance materials are the only authoritative source of information and should always be referred to for definitive guidance.

Pearson examiners have not contributed to any sections in this resource relevant to examination papers for which they have responsibility.

Examiners will not use endorsed resources as a source of material for any assessment set by Pearson.

Endorsement of a resource does not mean that the resource is required to achieve this Pearson qualification, nor does it mean that it is the only suitable material available to support the qualification, and any resource lists produced by the awarding body shall include this and other appropriate resources.

> **For the full range of Pearson revision titles across KS2, KS3, GCSE, Functional Skills, AS/A Level and BTEC visit:**
> www.pearsonschools.co.uk/revise

Contents

....

A small bit of small print

Edexcel publishes Sample Assessment Material and the Specification on its website. This is the official content and this book should be used in conjunction with it. The questions in *Now try this* have been written to help you practise every topic in the book. Remember: the real exam questions may not look like this.

Crime in Medieval England

The medieval period covers the end of the Anglo-Saxon era, Norman England and later Medieval England. Across all three eras there were some actions that have always been regarded as crimes, such as theft and murder.

What makes something a crime?

A 'crime' is an activity that breaks a law. Laws are made by the people who govern a country. During the Anglo-Saxon period the people who made the laws were the people with power and wealth. Crimes that threatened this authority and wealth were considered serious and were harshly punished. The more serious the crime, the harsher the punishment.

For more on medieval punishments, see page 5.

Crimes against the person	Crimes against property	Crimes against authority
• Murder • Assault • Public disorder • Rape	• Arson • Theft, such as stealing crops or poaching • Counterfeiting coins	• Treason • Rebellion
Varying from fairly serious (assault) to serious (rape and murder).	Varying from not serious (petty theft or selling poor quality goods) to very serious (arson).	All seen as extremely serious.

The king as law maker

Many laws in Anglo-Saxon times were still based on local custom and were not written down. However, by 1000 Anglo-Saxon kings were issuing codes of law that made certain actions crimes, illustrating the growing power of the monarch. This meant that laws were becoming more unified across the country. After 1066, the importance of the king in making laws grew as his authority increased. William I added new laws that created new crimes, illustrating how a powerful king can lead to change. In the later medieval period, the monarch continued to play a vital role in defining what a crime was. After Henry II became king in 1154, standard laws were written down, meaning that, for the first time, there was a uniform legal system across the whole country.

For more about new crimes, see page 2.

Poaching

Hunting wild animals on other people's land without paying 'hunting rights' is known as poaching. It's a form of theft that increased dramatically after the Forest Laws, as peasants used what had previously been common land to catch animals for food. It is seen as a 'social' crime because it was considered to be acceptable to many people – catching animals for food on common land was allowed and helped people survive. Reducing the amount of common land meant many had to choose between breaking the law and going hungry.

For more on the Forest Laws, see page 2.

The other huge authority in defining criminal activity across the medieval period was the Church. The Church created laws that criminalised some actions, influenced the types of punishment given in response and played a direct role in deciding guilt or innocence.

For more on the role of the Church, see page 6.

Now try this

Define each of the following terms and give **one** example of each:
(a) crimes against the person (b) crimes against property (c) crimes against authority.

'New' crimes in Norman England

After the Norman conquest in 1066, King William I wanted to establish his royal authority over his new kingdom. One of the ways he did this was by adding new crimes to the existing Anglo-Saxon ones, such as rebellion, and those covered by the Forest Laws and the Murdrum fine.

William 1's Forest Laws

About 30% of England became 'Royal Forest', which William I and the Norman nobility used for hunting.

Village communities and farms were evicted from this land, which caused resentment.

The Royal Forests were protected by new Forest Laws.

Only those people who paid for hunting rights were allowed to hunt in the Royal Forest.

In the Royal Forests it became illegal to graze animals, kill wild animals or take wood without a licence.

The Forest Laws were seen as unfair by ordinary people so those who broke these laws were not seen as criminals by most people in society.

Rebellions

The Norman invasion was not welcomed by the Anglo-Saxons and there was much resistance for the first few years, including large rebellions in York and East Anglia. Betraying your lord and inciting rebellion against a king had been crimes in Anglo-Saxon times, but William I punished these crimes far more harshly to try to assert his authority. As would have been done in Anglo-Saxon times, William ordered the death penalty for the rebels themselves. What was different was that William also punished those who were not directly involved in the rebellions – estimates suggest that 100 000 people starved to death due to the destruction of farmland and animals on William's orders in the areas that had seen rebellions.

Murdrum fine

This new law was used to help establish control over the conquered population. If an Anglo-Saxon murdered a Norman, and the culprit was not caught, a large sum of money had to be paid by the **hundred** where the body was found. In this way, murdering a Norman became a more serious crime than murdering an Anglo-Saxon, which is another example of how the ruling classes can make laws to benefit themselves.

Key term

Hundred – an area of land.

Now try this

Give **three** reasons why ordinary people hated the Forest Laws.

 To answer this question, look at this page and at page 4.

Anglo-Saxon law enforcement

Throughout medieval times there was <u>no official 'police force'</u>. During the Anglo-Saxon period, the community was largely <u>responsible for both preventing crime and catching criminals.</u>

Anglo-Saxon society

Around the <u>year 1000</u>, most people lived in <u>small hamlets or on farms, or in villages and a few small towns</u> (burhs). In these small, tight-knit communities <u>everyone knew everyone else</u> and most people had a <u>strong sense of duty towards thei</u>r <u>community</u>. This was an <u>important reason why the crime rate was fairly low and had an impact on how the law was enforced.</u>

An Anglo-Saxon burh.

> The <u>Church played a huge role in medieval</u> <u>law enforcement – see page 6 for details.</u>

For more on Anglo-Saxon punishments, see page 5.

Anglo-Saxon law enforcement

Tithings: Shires were split into areas called hundreds and each hundred was divided <u>into ten **tithings**, All men</u> <u>in a tithing were responsible for each other: if one was accused of a crime, the others made sure he went to</u> <u>court or they would have to pay a fine for him</u>. A **shire reeve** (later the sheriff) was a local man appointed by the community to take criminals to courts and make sure any punishment was carried out. He also met regularly with one man from each tithing.

⬇

Hue and cry: <u>The victim or a witness to a crime raised a hue and cry</u> <u>by shouting to alert others.</u> Anyone who heard the hue and cry was expected to chase and help catch the suspected criminal.

⬇

Courts: <u>If the suspect did not admit to the crime, or was not caught in the act, their guilt or innocence</u> had to be decided by a court. There were <u>different courts depending on the type of crime committed and the</u> <u>person who committed it</u> – <u>royal courts were national courts that dealt with the most serious of crimes;</u> <u>lesser crimes were dealt with in shire courts; and petty crimes were dealt with in hundred courts</u>. Court hearings, in which the punishment that convicted criminals would receive was decided, took place in public.

⬇

Oaths: <u>Swearing oaths 'before God' was a major part of Anglo-Saxon justice. The accused could swear their</u> <u>innocence under oath and others could support them as 'oath helpers'.</u>

⬇

Deciding guilt or innocence: The victim or their family <u>provided evidence of the suspect's guilt for the</u> <u>court. If the jury couldn't decide, the accused was handed over to the Church so God could decide a person's</u> <u>guilt or innocence in a trial by ordeal.</u>

Now try this

Why was Anglo-Saxon law enforcement mainly the responsibility of local communities?

Norman and later medieval law enforcement

After 1066, the Normans kept much of the Anglo-Saxon system of law enforcement. There were more changes in later medieval times that saw the start of the move towards the authorities being more responsible for enforcing the law.

Norman law enforcement

Continuity: The Anglo-Saxon system of tithings, the hue and cry and the court system continued. Law enforcement in most cases remained the responsibility of the community.

Change: The Normans introduced trial by combat (showing the more military nature of Norman society) as another way of settling disputes. The two people involved would fight until one was killed or surrendered (and he would then be put to death anyway).

Another change was the use of 'foresters' to police the Royal Forests and enforce Forest Laws. They dealt with suspects very harshly and were often feared and hated by the local communities.

The Normans built castles in every part of England. They were designed to represent the strong royal authority and help impose law and order.

Later medieval law enforcement

As towns grew through the 13th and 14th centuries, so did crime. Although communities were still involved in law enforcement, the authorities became more involved through the appointment of officials.

Parish constables

- ✓ These were local people nominated by the community.
- ✓ It was an unpaid position. Constables did their usual jobs as well.
- ✓ They held the post for a year.

Role of local communities	Role of government-appointed officials
Continuity: The hue and cry system continued, as did tithings. **Change:** From the 1250s, parish constables led the chase for the criminal after the hue and cry was given and tried to keep the peace. They arrested suspects. **Change:** Some towns also had a night watch, in which volunteers patrolled the streets. Any suspected criminals they caught were handed over to the constable. **Continuity:** If juries were not able to reach a verdict, trial by ordeal and by combat continued to be used by communities as informal methods of law enforcement. **Change:** Trial by ordeal and by combat were abolished in 1215.	**Change:** Knights were appointed by Richard I as keepers of the peace in some 'unruly' areas from 1195. In 1327, Edward II extended this system to all areas. **Change:** Following the Justices of the Peace Act (1361), the role of keeper of the peace evolved to become Justice of the Peace. JPs had the power to hear minor crimes in small courts four times a year. They were still appointed by the monarch and were mostly local lords. **Change:** The role of the sheriff expanded. He was now expected to track down criminals if the hue and cry hadn't worked. From 1285, he was allowed to form a posse of local men to help chase and catch criminals.

Now try this

List at least **two** ways in which law enforcement differed in the later medieval period from the Norman period.

Medieval punishments

The aims of medieval punishment were **retribution**, **deterrence** and to keep people safe. Although these aims remained largely the same throughout this period, the types of punishment changed.

Types of punishment

Fines

Stocks
(humiliation)

Maiming
(corporal)

Flogging
(corporal)

Hanging
(capital)

Beheading
(capital)

Changes in types of medieval punishment

Anglo-Saxon	Norman	Later medieval
• Fines and compensation were most common. • The system of paying compensation to victims of crime was used for many crimes, including murder. This was called the Saxon Wergild. • **Corporal punishments** were also fairly common but **capital punishment** was rarely used.	• Use of capital and corporal punishments rose dramatically. More offences became capital crimes. • Breaking Forest Laws was punished very harshly, including castration, blinding and hanging. • The Wergild system was ended and fines were paid to the king. • Very minor crimes were still punished by fines, whipping or time in the stocks.	• Use of capital punishment gradually decreased, although crimes against authority were still harshly punished. • Corporal punishments were still widely used, although many juries would not convict their neighbours unless they regularly offended. • Fines became more common.

The Church influenced punishment during both the Anglo-Saxon and later Middle Ages. It wanted the aim of punishment to involve reforming the criminal.

Social status and punishment

Medieval punishments varied depending on class and gender – commoners were treated differently to nobles, women differently to men and priests differently to ordinary people. Good examples of this include the following.

• The amount of Wergild payable in Anglo-Saxon times depended on the victim's social status. Wergild for nobles was a huge sum, whereas Wergild for a serf was very little.

• During the later medieval period, commoners were usually hanged for murder while nobles were usually beheaded.

Norman punishments

The Norman invasion was not welcomed by the Anglo-Saxons and there was much resistance for the first few years. Harsh punishments carried out in public were seen by the Normans as the best way to make people behave.

Key terms

Capital punishment – killing the criminal.
Corporal punishment – physically hurting the criminal.
Retribution – making a criminal suffer for the crime committed.
Deterrence – trying to prevent others or the criminal from carrying out crime.

Now try this

Give **three** similarities between Anglo-Saxon, Norman and later medieval punishments.

The influence of the Church

🔍 **Case study** Throughout this period the Church was extremely powerful and played a direct role in deciding what constituted a crime, how the accused was tried and what punishments were handed out. In the early 13th century there was change and continuity in the Church's role.

Benefit of clergy

Throughout the 13th century Church courts were used to try people accused of moral crimes, such as sex outside marriage, and not following Church rites.

Church courts also tried members of the clergy for all crimes. This was known as **benefit of clergy**. People proved their right to benefit of clergy by reading a passage from the Bible – priests were some of the few members of society who could read. Many laymen memorised the passage so they could recite it in court and claim benefit of clergy. This was because punishments given by Church courts were generally more lenient than those given by other courts, as the Church wanted to give people the chance to reform.

The significance of benefit of clergy is that it illustrates how the justice system in medieval society was not equal – it provided a way for people to be treated differently. Notably, benefit of clergy was not available to women as women couldn't be priests.

Sanctuary

✓ Sanctuary (protection from the law) was offered by some important churches only.

✓ A person could claim sanctuary by going to one of these churches.

✓ The priest would report the crime but no one was allowed to arrest the accused.

✓ The accused could either agree to go to court or swear an oath agreeing to leave the country.

✓ If the accused had not left the country within 40 days, they would be outlawed.

Sanctuary and benefit of clergy were significant because they showed how the Church operated an alternative justice system outside the control of other authorities.

The church was the focal point of all medieval villages and towns.

Trial by ordeal

Trial by ordeal was first used in Anglo-Saxon times but was still being used at the start of the 13th century. In cases where a person's guilt or innocence could not be decided by a court, the Church used a trial by ordeal. Various methods were used but the outcome of all these trials was seen as God's judgement on the guilt or innocence of the accused. In 1215, the pope ordered his priests to stop administering these trials and they quickly ended.

Trial by hot water or iron (if the burn healed well the person was innocent).

Trial by water (if the person sank they were innocent).

Trial by consecrated bread (for priests only, if they choked they were guilty).

Now try this

Give **three** ways in which Church courts were used in the 13th century.

Crime in early modern England

There were huge social and religious changes in England between c1500 and c1700. These changes led to changes in the nature of crimes against the person, property and authority. What had been classified as a crime in medieval times also continued into this period.

Changes in society		Led to increase in crimes against:
Increase in population and decline of feudalism led to higher unemployment, which meant more people moved to urban areas in search of work, so towns and cities grew.		The person, with the increase of street criminals and petty thieves.
The end of feudalism and new farming methods led to enclosure of land (fencing it off for the exclusive use of the landowner).		Property, for example poaching, as more landowners restricted those who could hunt on their land.
Changes in people's religious beliefs and the religion of the monarch.		Authority, as more people committed **heresy** and **high treason**.

Increase in crimes against authority

Early modern England was ruled by the Tudors and then the Stuarts. It was a time of religious change and many rebellions and plots against the monarch, both of which led to an increase in crimes against authority – heresy and treason.

Treason charges were more common in this period because there were more disputes about who should rule. Heresy charges were more common because the official religion of the country kept changing from Catholic to Protestant to Catholic, then back to Protestant! Important members of the clergy (both Catholic and Protestant at different times) played a role in charging people with heresy and also in judging whether they were guilty or not. As monarchs (except for Mary I) became the head of the Church, heresy and treason became interlinked.

Heresy first became a crime in 1382. As both the Church and monarch felt threatened by different beliefs, heresy was classed as a crime against authority and therefore usually punished by being burned to death at the stake.

Timeline

Treason and heresy

1547–53 Edward VI executed leaders of rebellions for treason and two Catholics for heresy.

1553–58 Mary I executed leaders of plots to replace her and many Protestants (almost 300) for heresy.

1603–25 James I executed many Catholics for treason.

1509–47 Henry VIII executed Protestants for heresy throughout his reign and Catholics for treason if they wouldn't accept Henry as head of the Church after 1534.

1158–1603 Elizabeth I executed many 'rebels' for treason but far fewer for heresy.

Key terms

High treason – the crime of plotting or acting to overthrow or harm the ruler or country.
Heresy – the crime of having religious beliefs that were different to the official religion of the country.

The Gunpowder Plot, a conspiracy to try to replace the monarch with another of a different religion, is an example of treason. For more on this, see page 11.

Now try this

Explain why there was an increase in charges of treason and heresy under the Tudors.

'New' crimes in early modern England

Huge changes in society were not just an important factor in changes to existing crimes, they also led to other activities being redefined as crimes.

Vagabondage or vagrancy

A vagabond, or vagrant, is an unemployed, homeless person. The late 15th and 16th centuries saw a large increase in the number of vagrants due to the increasing population, falling wages, rising food prices and no system to help the needy (especially after the closure of the monasteries in 1536).

Hated and feared by settled population.

Resorted to thieving and/or begging and charity in order to survive, which was resented by the settled population.

Viewed as lazy and responsible for their own problems.

Vagrant in early modern England.

Timeline

Vagabondage laws

1494 Vagabonds and Beggars Act – vagabonds were put in stocks for three days and nights, then sent back to where they were born or most well-known.

1547 Vagrancy Act – the able-bodied without work for more than three days were branded with the letter 'v' and sold as a slave for two years. (Repealed as it was impossible to enforce.)

1597 Act for the Relief of the Poor – split vagrants into two categories: 'deserving' (elderly and disabled) and 'undeserving' (those fit for work).

1601 Poor Laws – the 'deserving' poor were given poor relief by the local parish; the 'undeserving' could be branded, whipped or sent to a correction house.

Laws were passed to make vagrancy a crime. This is an example of how the general population can put pressure on government to make laws on what they feel should be classed as a crime.

Smuggling

When import tax on certain goods, including brandy and tea, was introduced in the 17th century, the crime of smuggling increased dramatically. Smuggling is where people bring goods into the country secretly to avoid paying import tax and then sell it on. Like poaching, it is an example of a social crime and many people did not view it as serious or a threat, making it very difficult to enforce.

Witchcraft

Witchcraft had been a minor crime in medieval times that was dealt with by Church courts. During the early modern period, new laws against witchcraft were passed, making it a very serious offence because people saw it as harmful and most were very afraid of it.

- In 1542, Henry VIII made witchcraft punishable by death.

- In 1563, Elizabeth I changed the law so charges of witchcraft had to be tried in a common court.

- In 1604, James I instructed the death penalty to be given to people 'summoning evil spirits'.

For more on witchcraft and the witch-hunts of 1645–47, see page 12.

Now try this

Give **three** reasons why vagrancy became a crime in early modern England.

Law enforcement in early modern England

The increasing size of the populations of towns was an important factor for changes in law enforcement. Traditional methods became less effective and a more organised system was put in place where town authorities and local communities both played a part. The role of the Church in the justice system decreased.

Continuity and change in catching criminals and preventing crime

As in medieval times, in early modern England:

- people were expected to raise and join the hue and cry to catch criminals when a crime took place

- there was no national police force and the methods and effectiveness of preventing crime and catching criminals varied widely across the country.

However, there were some changes to the roles of town constables and watchmen to try to deal with increased urban crime.

Changes in the role of the Church

In the Middle Ages, the Church provided an alternative justice system through benefit of clergy and sanctuary. The early modern period saw the justice system become far more secular as the Church itself became less important in society.

Benefit of clergy: Henry VII allowed non-clergy 'benefit of clergy' only once and people were branded to show they had received the privilege. Edward VI made serious crimes, such as murder, exempt from benefit of clergy. From 1576 Church courts couldn't try criminal acts (only moral ones) so everyone, including clerics, were tried in secular courts. People could still claim benefit of clergy and receive more lenient sentences than others, however.

Sanctuary: Henry VIII stopped exile abroad for those claiming sanctuary. Instead they had to keep to designated sanctuaries in England. In 1623, James I abolished sanctuary altogether.

For more on benefit of clergy and sanctuary, see page 6.

Watchmen

1. Carried a lamp to light their way.
2. Rang a bell to alert people.
3. All male householders were expected to volunteer and role was unpaid.
4. Patrolled the streets between 10pm and dawn.
5. Overseen by town constable.

Town constables

1. Employed by authorities in towns.
2. Respected members of the community.
3. Had the power to arrest suspects and take them to the Justice of the Peace.
4. In charge of the watchmen in their area.
5. Helped with town administration.

Now try this

List **three** ways local communities were responsible for enforcing the law in early modern England.

Punishment in early modern England

Capital and corporal methods continued to be the most common forms of punishment in this period. In fact, many more capital offences were introduced, as well as a new form of punishment: transportation.

Continuity in aims and types of punishment

Fines: These continued to be used to punish minor crimes.

Pillory or stocks, flogging or maiming: These forms of corporal punishment continued for crimes, such as begging, drunkenness and vagrancy.

Hanging: Capital punishment was still commonly used for crimes, such as theft, murder and poaching, and also witchcraft and smuggling. Nobles were beheaded rather than hanged.

Burning: This was used only as a punishment for heresy.

Retribution and deterrence were still the main purpose of punishments at this time.

Heretics being burned to death in London, 1546.

The Bloody Code

Change: In the 17th century the number of crimes punishable by death increased. By 1688 there were 50 capital offences ranging from what today seem like minor crimes, such as stealing a rabbit or loaf of bread, to murder. Because of the increase in capital offences, the period from 1688 to 1825 became known as the 'Bloody Code'. The aim was to frighten people so they wouldn't commit crime.

For more on the Bloody Code and its end, see pages 13, 16 and 18.

Transportation to North America

Change: Transporting criminals to colonies in North America, where they did manual work, began under James I (1603–25). Criminals were sentenced to either seven or 14 years and were then released but most could not afford to return to England. Between 50 000 and 80 000 men, women and children were transported to America during this time. Transportation became a punishment because:

- it reflected new ideas on the aims of punishment – transportation was still a serious punishment but gave criminals a chance at rehabilitation while still acting as a deterrent
- it provided an alternative to execution for petty crime which some began to think was too harsh, especially after the Bloody Code began and when prisons were not yet established
- it provided inhabitants and workers to establish the American colonies while removing criminals from England.

For more on transportation, see page 16.

Now try this

Outline the purposes of punishment for crimes during the early modern period.

The Gunpowder Plotters, 1605

Case study The Gunpowder Plotters received the harshest punishment for committing what was seen by the authorities as the worst crime of all: treason.

The Plot

After 1570, when the pope called on Catholics to depose Elizabeth I, more laws were imposed that prevented Catholics from practising their faith. When the reign of the Tudors ended with Elizabeth's death in 1603, her cousin's son, James Stuart, inherited the throne. Catholics hoped for more freedom to practise their faith.

The Houses of Parliament in the 17th century.

But James I continued with anti-Catholic laws. A group of Catholics, led by Robert Catesby, plotted to kill the king and other leading Protestants at the state opening of parliament on 5 November 1605. The plotters wanted to make James' daughter, Elizabeth, queen.

Lord Monteagle gave a letter he received on 30 October 1605, which warned him not to attend the state opening of parliament, to Robert Cecil (James I's spymaster).

The plotters rented a house next to, and a cellar directly underneath, the Houses of Parliament. They filled the cellar with barrels of gunpowder.

Cecil ordered a search of the Houses of Parliament. The gunpowder and Guy Fawkes were dicovered on 5 November. Guy Fawkes was arrested and, after torture, gave up the names of his fellow conspirators. Those captured were arrested and also tortured until they confessed.

The plotters being hanged.

The plotters were tried and found guilty of treason in January 1606. They were publicly hanged, drawn and quartered on 30–31 January 1606.

Reasons for harsh and public punishment for treason

1 As the most serious crime, treason received the most serious punishment.

2 Without a police force to help prevent crime, harsh punishment was thought to be the only way of deterring crime.

3 The period of political instability, due to disputes over the royal succession, required harsh treatment as a form of deterrent.

4 A harsh message was thought necessary to deter Catholics from rising up against the Protestant monarchy.

Now try this

Explain why the Gunpowder Plotters were publicly hanged, drawn and quartered.

The witch-hunts of 1645–47

🔍 **Case study** The years 1645–47 saw a huge increase in the number of executions for witchcraft in England. Many of these were due to Matthew Hopkins, who called himself the 'Witchfinder General'.

What were the witch-hunts?

'Witch-hunts' were when people actively tried to discover witches. The hunts of 1645–47 occurred during the English Civil War (1642–51), a period of great upheaval. They were concentrated in certain areas, particularly the east of England. Hundreds of women and a few men (mostly clergymen) were investigated. Those convicted were executed, usually by hanging.

The frontispiece of Matthew Hopkins' pamphlet, *The discovery of witches*, published in 1647. The invention of the printing press in 1440 meant that information was spread more quickly.

See page 10 for the laws which made witchcraft a serious crime in the early modern period.

Social changes
The war left many women widowed or on their own as their husbands went away to fight. Also, there were more 'strangers' around as people travelled with the armies or searched for work.

Economic problems
The Civil War and poor harvests caused huge economic problems. People looked for scapegoats.

Lack of authority
Civil War weakened the control of local authorities. In some areas law and order collapsed completely.

Reasons for the intensity of the 1645–47 witch-hunts

James I's book, *Demonologie*, outlined his belief in witches and how they should be found and tried. He was very superstitious and encouraged witch-hunts. These ideas were still around for many years after his death in 1625.

Religious change
Religious differences were increased by the Civil War. Many Puritans, on the side of parliament, believed that witchcraft was being used by the Royalists, some of whom were Catholic.

Influence of individuals
Since 1603, James I had promoted witch-hunting. People like Matthew Hopkins stirred up fear of witches through their writings, as well as actually taking part in witch-hunts themselves.

Matthew Hopkins

 Hopkins was employed by a Justice of the Peace to find witches in Essex and East Anglia.

 He received money for each person prosecuted for being a witch. It's estimated that his 'work' led to around 300 people being investigated for witchcraft, with 112 of these hanged.

✓ He used torture to extract confessions, which often included the names of other witches for him to investigate.

✓ He helped stir up mass panic and fear of witches during the years 1645–47 through his prosecutions and pamphlets.

Evidence of witchcraft

The following were all used as evidence to convict people of witchcraft.

1. Unusual marks on the body of the person accused.
2. Witness accounts.
3. When pricked with a needle the accused doesn't bleed.
4. When thrown in water the accused floats.
5. Confessions from the accused.
6. If two proven witches swear the accused is a witch.
7. 'Possessed' children acting as accusers.

Now try this

Give **three** ways in which the English Civil War helped lead to the witch-hunts of 1645–47.

Crimes against the person and property

There were few brand-new crimes against the person or property in this period, but a great deal of change in the ways in which these crimes were committed, which led to changes in the law. Another change was in the crime rate, which rose dramatically. This was due to a rise in crimes against property.

Factors causing increased crime

The period 1700 to around 1850 saw an increase in crimes, such as street theft and burglary; drunk and disorderly behaviour; prostitution and public disorder. Reasons for this included:

- people travelling more and moving into towns meant that fewer people knew each other and communities were less tightly knit
- larger towns that made it easier to escape being caught
- some criminals became 'professional' within dens or gangs of thieves
- extreme poverty that led to a rise in 'survival' crimes, such as stealing food.

In 1772, to try to reduce highway robbery, it became a capital crime to be armed and in disguise on a high road. Mounted patrols on major roads and the growth of the railways helped reduce instances of highway robbery, which disappeared completely in the 1830s.

Changes in highway robbery – a crime against the person

Highway robbery increased in the 18th century because:

- improved roads led to more people travelling,
- increased trade between towns meant more goods and money were transported by road,
- many roads were isolated, making it easy to get away with highway robbery.

The famous highwaymen, Dick Turpin and Tom King, at work. Turpin, like many highway robbers and smugglers, was often seen as a hero despite committing many violent crimes.

Changes in poaching – a crime against property

Poaching increased in the 18th century, with poaching gangs that worked on a large scale. This led to the 1723 Waltham Black Act, which made poaching a capital crime and also made it illegal to carry snares or own hunting dogs in a poaching area. Many viewed this law as unfair. Many poaching laws were repealed in 1823.

Laws making poaching and highway robbery capital crimes were part of the Bloody Code. For more on the Bloody Code, see pages 10, 16 and 18.

Changes in smuggling – a crime against property

Smuggling increased from 1740–1850 because the tax on imported goods was so high. Smugglers made large profits by bringing these goods into the country without paying tax and selling them on. This led to large gangs of smugglers, such as the Hawkhurst Gang, which smuggled huge volumes of goods. Mounted customs officers tried to prosecute smugglers. They found it dificult because of the large areas of coast to patrol. Taxes were cut in the 1840s and smuggling decreased.

Many people thought smugglers were heroes who brought them cheap goods. They thought the government was being unreasonable. Lots of people were involved in smuggling:

- the smugglers themselves
- those who traded with smugglers
- those who bought smuggled goods
- those who gave smugglers alibis.

Now try this

Describe **two** different attitudes to highwaymen in 18th century society. Give **two** reasons for the decline in highway robbery in the 19th century.

Crimes against authority

There were many changes to crimes against authority in this period. Some activities, such as witchcraft, ceased to be crimes. Charges of treason fell in this period also, but the government found other ways of dealing with those they viewed as a challenge to their authority.

Witchcraft

After the Civil War the number of prosecutions of witchcraft declined. All laws concerning witchcraft were appealed by the Witchcraft Act of 1736. People who claimed to use magic were subject to fines or imprisonment. However, although most people's attitudes and the attitude of the authorities had changed, some still clung to their superstitious beliefs.

Why witchcraft stopped being a crime

- ✓ Economic and social changes led to more prosperity and political stability.
- ✓ Some still believed in witches and the Devil, but others (especially the educated) became less superstitious.
- ✓ The Royal Society, set up by Charles II, led to increased scientific experiments, which explained things previously thought to be the work of witches.

The Tolpuddle Martyrs

In 1834, in Tolpuddle, Dorset, a group of farm workers formed a 'friendly society' (an early form of trade union) to protest about their low wages compared to other farm workers' wages.

↓

The farm owners and the government feared they were losing control of their workers. The six men were arrested for taking secret oaths – an old law intended to stop Naval mutinies.

↓

The six were found guilty at their trial. They all received the maximum sentence of seven years transportation to Australia in an attempt to deter others from forming trade unions.

↓

News of the Tolpuddle Martyrs' sentences spread quickly due to the press. There were mass protests and a petition of 200000 signatures collected in opposition of their harsh punishment.

↓

The Home Secretary decided to continue their sentence and the six were sent to Australia.

↓

Protests continued and in 1836 the martyrs were pardoned and returned home.

Significance of the Tolpuddle Martyrs

- The incident highlights how authorities used laws to criminalise people they viewed as a threat.
- It shows how the government would protect the interests of employers at the expense of workers.
- The pardoning of the martyrs illustrates the impact of public opinion.
- The martyrs inspired some to fight for workers' rights but others were put off by how the martyrs were treated.

Four of the six Tolpuddle Martyrs transported to Australia for the crime of setting up a trade union. The six martyrs were George Loveless and his brother James, Thomas Standfield and his son John, James Hammett and James Brine.

Now try this

What were the authorities trying to achieve by giving the Tolpuddle Martyrs such harsh sentences?

Law enforcement

Industrialisation and urbanisation were major factors that increased the crime rate after 1700, and created a need for better law enforcement. As a consequence, this period saw the development of more official forms of policing.

Continuity and change in policing

Watchmen continued to patrol cities on foot at night and parish constables dealt with petty crime. Soldiers were used to put down riots and large protests across the country. There were some changes in London though as, from 1749, the Bow Street Runners tracked down criminals and stolen property. From 1754 the Bow Street Horse Patrols patrolled the streets.

The Bow Street Runners catching criminals, 1806.

The Bow Street Runners

- Established in London in 1749 by Henry Fielding, Chief Magistrate at Bow Street Court, to try to tackle the huge crime wave of 17th-century London. Fielding's half-brother, John, took over in 1754.

- At first they charged fees and collected rewards, but by 1785 they were paid by the government.

- Introduced new methods of finding evidence to bring criminals to justice – the first modern 'detectives'.

- Branched out to patrolling major roads both on foot and horse (mounted patrols). The patrols were less successful than the detecting side, as there were not enough of them to deal with the dramatically increasing crime rate.

- Shared information on crimes and suspects with others – the beginnings of a crime intelligence network.

Timeline

Development of police forces, 1829–1900

1829 Metropolitan Police Act – began Britain's first professional police force in London.

1835 Municipal Corporations Act – borough councils could set up police forces in their area (but only around half did so).

1839 Rural Constabulary Act – countries could set up police forces, which two-thirds of the counties did.

1842 Detective department set up at the Metropolitan Police Force headquarters in London.

1856 Police Act – forced all towns and counties to set up a professional police force.

1878 Criminal Investigations Department (CID) set up for the Metropolitan Police Force.

The setting up of the Metropolitan Police Force (also known as 'the Met') was largely the work of Robert Peel. For more details on Peel and the Met, see page 18.

The 1856 Police Act

This act made professional police forces, which were based on the model of the Metropolitan Police, compulsory across the whole country. All forces were funded by the government and were regularly inspected by officials employed by the government. Police officers were not only tasked with keeping law and order, preventing crime through patrolling the streets and arresting criminals, but were to detect criminals after crimes had been committed. The aim of all activities was to deter crime.

Now try this

Explain why the work of the Fielding brothers was a significant advance in policing.

Changing views on the purpose of punishment

The period saw a change in attitudes to the purpose of punishment. Transportation and public executions stopped and imprisonment as a punishment increased.

Timeline

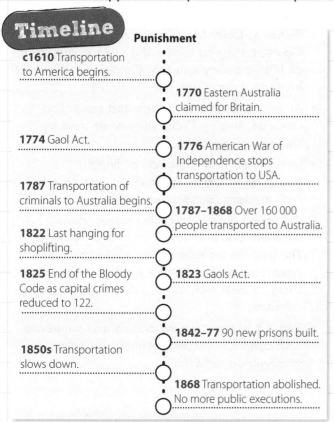

Punishment

c1610 Transportation to America begins.

1770 Eastern Australia claimed for Britain.

1774 Gaol Act.

1776 American War of Independence stops transportation to USA.

1787 Transportation of criminals to Australia begins.

1787–1868 Over 160 000 people transported to Australia.

1822 Last hanging for shoplifting.

1825 End of the Bloody Code as capital crimes reduced to 122.

1823 Gaols Act.

1842–77 90 new prisons built.

1850s Transportation slows down.

1868 Transportation abolished. No more public executions.

Factors that changed views on the purpose of punishment

Rapidly growing crime rates led the government to increase the Bloody Code throughout the 18th century. The number of capital crimes reached a peak of 222 in 1810 in an attempt to deter crime. However, it was clear that these deterrents were not working and a new strategy was needed. Continuing the idea that punishment should be about retribution and deterrence, the 19th century saw increasing feelings that:

- punishments should be equal to the crime committed
- corporal and capital punishments were inhumane except for very serious crimes
- punishment should also be about rehabilitating the offender.

This led to a decrease in the use of the death penalty and the end of the Bloody Code and an increase in other forms of punishment: firstly transportation and then imprisonment. This change in attitude also helped lead to the ending of public executions in 1868.

Transportation to Australia

The increase in the crime rate increased transportation to Australia. Once there the criminals worked for settlers for seven years providing free labour to build infrastructure. Most stayed in Australia once their sentence ended as they couldn't afford the fare home. Transportation ended by 1868 because:

- Australia no longer needed forced labourers (the discovery of gold made it an attractive place to go) and it didn't want 'criminals'.
- Some felt it was too expensive and not a strong enough deterrent to crime. Others felt it was too harsh for both the criminals and their families.
- More prisons had been built and prison was increasingly used instead of transportation.

For more on the reasons why transportation took place, see page 10.

Prisons and prison reformers

Conditions in 18th century prisons were very poor but they were increasingly used as a form of punishment. Many thought prison conditions should be poor with hard labour, but several reformers believed prisons should be improved to increase the likelihood of rehabilitation.

John Howard's work led to the 1774 Gaol Act, which suggested how health and sanitation in prisons could be improved. Elizabeth Fry began visiting women in Newgate Prison in 1813. She set up education classes to reform female prisoners. She also got them better food and clothes, and treated prisoners with kindness and respect.

Their work influenced Peel's prison reforms.

See page 18 for more on Peel and penal and prison reform and page 17 for an example of how new prison rules were applied to Pentonville Prison.

Now try this

Describe how attitudes towards punishment changed during the period 1750–1900.

 You will need to know about changing attitudes.

Pentonville Prison

🔍 **Case study** Pentonville Prison was built in 1842. It was a model for a new idea about how prisons should be run and prisoners treated – it was known as the separate system.

Pentonville – the 'model' prison

The wings housed dozens of individual cells and a staff base. Walls were very thick to prevent prisoners talking to each other.

Areas where prisoners were sent for fresh air and exercise. They were masked to prevent communication.

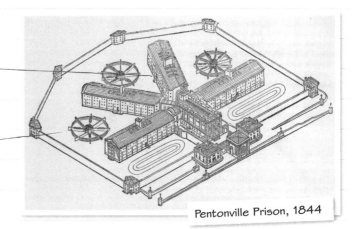

Pentonville Prison, 1844

Each cell was 4m x 2m

Loom for working on

Small, barred window

Wash basin and a toilet

Bed, mattress and blanket

A cell in Pentonville Prison, 1862.

Prison chapel in 1862. It had individual cubicles so prisoners couldn't see each other.

Prisoners undertook monotonous and repetitive work that, to begin with, was done in their cells.

Reasons for the separate system

1. For rehabilitation: Solitude was thought to be the best way to provide prisoners with an opportunity to reflect on their crimes, turn to religion and therefore reform their ways. It also meant that prisoners could not be influenced by other criminals. The cell provided everything they needed so they didn't have to leave it other than for short spells of exercise.

2. For retribution: The isolation and boredom made the criminal 'pay' for their crime.

3. As a deterrent: It was a serious punishment and was therefore thought to act as a deterrent to committing crimes.

Strengths of the separate system

👍 Compared to previous prisons, it was clean and there was far less disease.

👍 Many people thought that it provided the right level of punishment – it was seen as harsh but not overly so.

Weaknesses of the separate system

👎 The continuous isolation led to mental illness and a high suicide rate.

👎 There was no education or instruction to provide new skills for prisoners to use when they were released.

Now try this

Give **three** examples of how the design of Pentonville Prison supported the separate system.

Robert Peel

> **Case study** Robert Peel had a huge influence on both punishment and law enforcement when Home Secretary during the 1820s. He ended the Bloody Code by reducing the number of death penalty offences and tried to reform the prison system. In 1829, he persuaded parliament to pass the Metropolitan Police Act, which set up the first professional police force in London.

Reforming the penal code

After 1810 there were an unprecedented number of capital crimes. According to the law, someone could receive the same punishment for murder as they could for petty theft – the death penalty.

Robert Peel, 1788–1850

In practice, the death penalty was rarely used for petty crime, as judges thought it was unfair, and transportation or prison was usually preferred, which meant the penal code made little sense. In 1825, Peel reduced the number of capital crimes by 100 because he wanted:

- less harsh punishments for petty crimes
- to try to reform petty criminals rather than kill them.

Prison reform

Partly due to the influence of reformers, such as Elizabeth Fry, Peel tried to improve conditions in prisons through persuading parliament to pass the 1823 Gaols Act which stated that:

- chaplains should regularly visit prisoners
- gaolers should be paid
- prisoners should not be put in chains.

There were no inspectors to enforce the act so the impact was limited.

The Metropolitan Police Act, 1829

In 1822, Peel set up a parliamentary committee to look into the issue of policing London, which helped him come up with the idea of a centralised police force across the whole city. The crime wave resulting from the economic downturn in 1826 helped Peel get the act through parliament.

Metropolitan Police officers

The central aim was to prevent crime and disorder and to be totally impartial and objective.

Recruits carefully selected and well trained. It was a full-time and fairly well-paid job.

Members had a uniform so they could be identified (and didn't look like soldiers).

Metropolitan Police officers (Peelers) patrolling a graveyard, 1829.

Members were usually unarmed and were trained to use minimum physical force only as a last resort.

Focused on patrolling areas where crime was high. Successfully reduced street crime and disorder.

Not popular at first, but soon recognised by the public as being honest and trustworthy.

Now try this

Give **three** reasons why the Metropolitan Police Force managed to reduce the crime rate.

Crime in modern Britain

As Britain has developed and changed since 1900, criminals have found new and different ways of committing 'old' crimes against the person, property and authority.

Continuity or change?

Some modern crimes may seem to show change from those committed in the past but there is a lot of continuity, too. For example, theft has always been a common crime. However, computers and modern transport have created new ways to steal. Violent crimes are nothing new either, but the weapons used in violent acts have changed. Other crimes that are sometimes seen as 'new' are often simply new versions of older crimes, such as drink-driving (driving a horse-drawn coach while drunk was made illegal in 1872).

A policeman questions a drunk man driving a cart in 1905.

The Peeler.—"See here, my man! your name's obliterated!"
The Jarvey.—"Ye lie! tis O'Brien!"

Cybercrime

Most cybercrimes (crime committed over the internet) are new versions of old crimes. For example, online theft, fraud (deceiving someone to get money) or extortion (using threats to get money from someone). What is new is the scale, as thousands of people can be targeted at once, and perpetrators of cybercrime can be overseas, which causes new problems for police.

Smuggling

Smuggling legal and illegal items without paying tax has happened for centuries. In modern Britain, goods such as cigarettes, alcohol and illegal drugs are smuggled into the country. There has also been a growth in people-trafficking (smuggling people into the country illegally and selling them for prostitution and forced labour, or in exchange for a fee). As in the past, some types of smuggling, such as smuggling cigarettes and alcohol, are seen by some as less serious social crimes.

Terrorism

Terrorism is not new but modern weapons, transport and communications mean that more ordinary people are at risk (though the risk is extremely low).
On 7 July 2005 four suicide bombers, who claimed to be members of Al Qaeda, attacked central London. Three bombs went off on underground trains and one on a bus. Fifty-two people were killed and around 770 injured.

The Gunpowder Plot is an older form of terrorism, see page 11 for more on this.

The bus attacked by a suicide bomber in London, July 2005.

Now try this

Give **three** examples of 'new' crimes that are actually 'old' crimes using different means.

'New' crimes in modern Britain

Some genuinely 'new' crimes have emerged since 1900. This is due to factors including changing social attitudes, such as race crimes, and crimes related to modern technology, such as computer-hacking.

Changing society

In the 20th century, Britain developed into a society that was:

- multicultural, containing people of different races and religions
- more equal, as the position of women changed.

As attitudes changed, new laws were needed to ensure that all people were treated fairly and equally. Similarly, some activities that had previously been illegal were decriminalised.

Multicultural Britain.

Timeline

1967 Sexual Offences Act – decriminalised homosexuality for men over 21.

1967 Abortion Act – decriminalised abortion in certain situations.

1968 Race Relations Act – illegal to discriminate against someone because of their race or ethnicity.

2005 Criminal Justice Act – allowed more severe sentences for hate crimes (against gay people or because of someone's race or religion).

2006 Racial and Religious Hatred Act – made spreading racial or religious hatred a crime.

As in the past new laws have been passed to deal with new crimes. Public pressure contributes towards making governments act to make these laws.

Race crime

The 1968 Race Relations Act and the 2006 Racial and Religious Hatred Act both made certain acts race crimes. However, the Criminal Justice Act of 2005 gave criminal courts the power to give more severe sentences for other crimes, such as assault or murder, if they are classed as 'hate' crimes. In other words, if a crime is committed against someone because of their race, religion or sexuality, the criminal can receive harsher punishments than if the crime was committed for another reason.

Drug crimes

Since the introduction of the Misuse of Drugs Act in 1971, taking or supplying some substances has been illegal in the UK. Drugs are classified according to how dangerous they are perceived to be. The criminalisation of drugs is controversial. Some think it's important for some drugs to be illegal to clarify that taking them is wrong, while others believe that drug-taking is a personal choice.

Driving offences

Many driving crimes are totally new due to the huge number of vehicles on today's roads and the technological advances of modern transport. For example:

- driving while under the influence of drugs
- driving without insurance, an MOT certificate or a valid driving licence
- speeding
- ignoring traffic lights, road signs, etc.
- driving while using a mobile phone.

It is now illegal to drive while using a mobile phone.

Now try this

Explain why (a) driving offences and (b) racial discrimination became crimes in the 20th century.

Law enforcement in modern Britain

Modern law enforcement continues to be a mixture of community-run and authority-based schemes, but it is the authorities, in the form of the police, that take on the greater role in solving and preventing crime.

Changes in policing

Much of modern policing is about preventing crime as well as catching criminals. The police work with different forces and other agencies across the UK and worldwide.

1 Motorised transport means that police can reach crimes faster. However, it also means fewer police officers on the street, which some people don't like.

2 Some police officers are now armed and look more like soldiers, which not everybody supports.

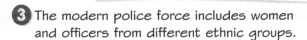

Armed police officers.

3 The modern police force includes women and officers from different ethnic groups.

Examples of special police units

Changes in technology and in the challenges police face have resulted in the development of specialisation to tackle specific types of crime. Some police officers specialise in dealing with certain crimes, such as rape, and specialist units have been set up including:

☑ **National Crime Agency (NCA)**: seeks to detect and prevent serious organised crime, including large-scale drug trafficking

☑ **Economic Crime Unit**: investigates large-scale fraud; officers require specialist understanding of financial systems

☑ **Police Central e-crime Unit (PCeU)**: tackles most serious types of cybercrimes and raises awareness on e-safety

☑ **Special Branch**: each local force has a Special Branch which aims to prevent all forms of terrorism.

Neighbourhood Watch

From 1982, Neighbourhood Watch groups have used volunteers to help prevent and detect crime in their neighbourhood. The idea was to increase vigilance and education to prevent crime, as well as reduce the fear of crime. It has met with varying degrees of success.

The move towards prevention

Much of modern policy is about preventing crime as well as catching criminals. Police Community Support Officers (PCSOs) were introduced in 2002 to try to prevent crime in their communities. The police work with schools and community groups, such as Neighbourhood Watch, to educate people to help protect themselves and their property. The police also play a major role in the government's Prevent programme, which aims to challenge extremism and radicalisation.

Use of science and technology

Rapid advances in technology have had a big impact on preventing, discovering and prosecuting crime since 1900.

Radios

DNA evidence

Computers

CCTV

Cars, motorbikes and helicopters

Finger printing

Now try this

For each item shown in the 'Use of science and technology' section, give an example of how this has helped the police since 1900.

Punishment in modern Britain

Methods of punishment in modern Britain are more diverse than ever before, and there has been considerable change since 1900.

Abolition of the death penalty

Capital punishment was last used in 1964. It was completely abolished in 1999 because:

- ideas about punishment continued to change – reform and paying back society were now considered more important

- controversial cases in the 1950s (Timothy Evans, Derek Bentley and Ruth Ellis, for example) led people to question the use of capital punishment.

> It's important to remember that many people didn't agree that capital punishment should be abolished.

Controversial cases

1950: Timothy Evans was hanged for murdering his wife and baby. Later evidence proved he didn't do it.

1953: Derek Bentley was hanged for murdering a policeman, even though he didn't fire the gun and had serious learning difficulties.

1955: Ruth Ellis was hanged for murdering her boyfriend after he had violently abused her for years.

For more on Derek Bentley, see page 24.

Prison

The use of prison as a punishment continued to increase after 1900 with many changes.

- Different prisons cater for different types of criminals. For example, there are open prisons where prisoners are not locked up in cells and, at the other extreme, high-security prisons where prisoners are kept in cells away from other inmates for most of the day.

- Since 1907, prisoners have been released on probation – they are watched by probation officers and put back in prison if they re-offend.

- In 1948 hard labour and corporal punishment in prisons were abolished.

- Separate 'prisons' have been established for young people. Borstals were set up in the early 1900s. They used work and education to try to reduce re-offending rates. Today's Young Offenders Institutions have high re-offending rates.

- There has been a recent rise in female prisoners, although still only 6% of all prisoners are women.

- Women's and men's prisons differ (e.g. women can spend more time with their children).

Inside Wormwood Scrubs, a Category B men's prison.

New punishments

New types of punishment have developed in the last two decades as non-custodial alternatives to prison. This means people are punished for their crime but not kept in prison.

- Community sentences – working on community projects, for example

- Antisocial Behaviour Orders (ASBOs)

- Electronic tagging

Rehabilitation

Prisons in the 1800s used to punish criminals to discourage them from re-offending on release. Prisons today try to reduce re-offending rates through education and giving prisoners work that teaches them new skills. However, they have mixed success rates, and the general public do not always support what can be portrayed as 'holiday camp' prisons.

Now try this

Give **five** examples of changes to punishment for criminals since 1900.

Conscientious objectors

 Case study Conscientious objectors are people who have religious, moral or political objections to war. For a short time in the 20th century, conscientious objection became a crime.

Conscription

Conscription is a law that states that everyone who is asked to, and who is fit and healthy, has to fight in the armed forces. Therefore, anyone who was conscripted but then refused to fight could be committing a crime. Conscription laws were introduced twice in Britain – during the First and Second World Wars. In both cases, conscientious objectors had to make their objections known to the authorities and were then tried by tribunals who judged whether their objections were genuine.

Attitudes to conscientious objectors

The punishment and treatment of conscientious objectors (COs) by the authorities was very different in the two world wars. This shows how people in authority changed their attitude. However, the attitude of the general public and treatment of conscientious objectors was fairly similar in both instances. This was probably because most people felt they and their families were making great sacrifices and that others should, too.

Different treatment by the authorities

First World War	Second World War
Conscription for men: from 1916.	Conscription: from April 1939 for men, from December 1941 for women.
A clause in law excused conscientious objectors.	A clause in law excused conscientious objectors.
About 16 000 men refused to fight.	Over 59 000 men and women refused to fight.
Military tribunals made up of military officers and professionals decided if CO was genuine.	Tribunals (minus military people) judged if CO was genuine.
Only 400 were given total exemption on grounds of conscience.	All except 12 204 were given complete or partial exemption.
'Alternativists' were given non-combatant roles.	Those with partial exemption were given non-combatant roles.
'Absolutists' were imprisoned, given brutal treatment and hard labour. Ten died in prison, 63 died after release and 31 had breakdowns.	A far smaller percentage of those not given exemption were sent to prison and those who did were not treated as harshly.

Similar treatment by the general public

During both wars, many members of the general public thought of conscientious objectors as cowards and traitors. Some COs were shouted at in the streets and were even physically abused. They and their families risked being shunned by former friends; many found it hard to get work and some were even dismissed from their jobs. However, there were some differences. The press was less harsh and there were fewer organised 'campaigns' against COs in the Second World War. During the First World War the organisation, The Order of the White Feather, encouraged women to hand out white feathers, symbolising cowardice, to young men not in military uniforms.

THE CONSCIENTIOUS OBJECTOR AT THE FRONT!

OH, YOU NAUGHTY UNKIND GERMAN— REALLY, IF YOU DON'T DESIST I'LL FORGET I'VE GOT A CONSCIENCE AND I'LL SMACK YOU ON THE WRIST!

A First World War postcard shows a CO as afraid to fight.

Now try this

Give **two** similarities and **two** differences in the treatment of conscientious objectors by the authorities during the First and Second World Wars.

The Derek Bentley case

Case study In 1953, Derek Bentley was hanged for murder. His was one of several controversial executions that played a part in the decision to abolish the death penalty.

Look back at page 22 for more on controversial executions.

The case of Derek Bentley

Derek Bentley (aged 19) had a learning disability and a mental age of 10. He and his friend, Christopher Craig (aged 16), decided to burgle a warehouse. The police arrived when they were on the roof so there was no escape.

Bentley was detained by DC Fairfax. Craig had a knife and a gun and shot DC Fairfax in the shoulder. According to Fairfax and two other policemen, Bentley later shouted, 'Let him have it, Chris', before Craig shot and killed PC Sidney Miles. When Craig ran out of bullets, he jumped off the roof and broke his back. Bentley stayed with the injured DC Fairfax.

Derek Bentley.

Detectives with evidence for the Bentley trial.

Both Bentley and Craig were tried and convicted of murder. Craig was sentenced to a long prison term as he was under 18. Bentley was sentenced to death by hanging. After a failed appeal hearing he was hanged on 28 January 1953.

Derek Bentley's family at the trial.

Public and parliamentary opinion

There was a huge public outcry against the sentence at the time. A motion in parliament to reprieve Bentley was supported by 200 MPs but it was never debated in parliament. The Home Secretary could have reprieved Bentley, as many others had been reprieved before, but chose not to.

The case received a lot of media coverage, mostly sympathetic to Bentley's cause. Derek Bentley's family continued the campaign after his death. He was pardoned in 1993 and in 1998 his conviction for murder was overturned.

Significance of the Bentley case

- ✓ It highlighted the vast differences in punishment for murder, as some were hanged while others were reprieved (and given prison sentences).

- ✓ It illustrated how the system of the Home Secretary reprieving murderers from hanging was a lottery.

- ✓ Combined with other controversial cases, it increased the number of people who were critical of the death penalty as a fair and just punishment.

Now try this

Explain why the Derek Bentley case was controversial.

The Metropolitan Police

The Metropolitan Police Force (the Met) was a government-directed police force policing the whole of London (except for the City of London, which had its own force). There needed to be cooperation between the Met and the City of London force when crimes occurred on the borders.

Police recruits for the Met

A Met constable, 1894.

- Most came from outside London and were attracted by the relatively good pay.

- Some had been soldiers but most had backgrounds in labouring or farm work.

- There were some problems with absenteeism and drinking on the job.

- By 1885, the Met totalled just 13 319 to police a population of over five million people. Only 1383 were on duty at a time.

Unlike other police forces, the Met was directly under the control of the Home Secretary. He appointed a commissioner to run the Metropolitan Police. The government wanted direct control of London's police force as it was worried about socialists and anarchists in some areas of London, such as Whitechapel.

For more on socialism in Whitechapel, see page 27.

The 'beat' constable

A major aim of the Met was to prevent crime. Its main way of doing this was to deploy constables on the 'beat' – patrolling a set route of streets to deter criminals from committing crime, asking people what they were doing and to break up fights and arrest suspects.

Development of the CID

The Criminal Investigation Department (CID) of the Met was set up in 1878. There had been a department to detect crime before this but it was quite ineffective. Those in the CID (to detect crime) were therefore separate from the rest of the force (to prevent crime), which clarified the roles of each. Initially the CID had little success, as shown by the investigation into the murders committed by Jack the Ripper in Whitechapel.

For more on investigative policing, see page 29.

Commissioner Sir Charles Warren

- Warren, a former army general, was appointed Met Commissioner in 1886.

- Warren banned a planned unemployment protest in Trafalgar Square on 13 November 1887. When the protestors ignored the ban, he deployed thousands of police, supported by about 1000 men from the army. Violent clashes followed, many people were injured and one protestor later died. Warren directed the operation from horseback.

- When Jack the Ripper struck in the autumn of 1888, in Whitechapel, Warren ordered an increase in patrols. Failure to catch the murderer cost Warren his job.

Attitudes towards the police

Attitudes varied widely. The police still had people's trust in some areas but events, such as the Trafalgar Square riot of 1887, contributed to the feeling held by many working-class people that the police were 'against' them, and only worked for the middle and upper classes. The economic depression and ensuing poverty of the period contributed to this hatred of police.

Mounted Met Police charge at protestors in Trafalgar Square during the Bloody Sunday riots, 13 November 1887.

Now try this

List at least **four** problems that the Metropolitan Police faced between 1870 and 1900.

The local context of Whitechapel

Whitechapel is an area of London just east of the City. In the late 1880s, this district had very high levels of poverty and poor living and working conditions, all of which contributed to a high crime rate.

Housing

'Rookeries' (slum areas) in Whitechapel, where most housing was located, were extremely overcrowded with poor sanitation.

Lodging houses, where lodgers paid a nightly fee for a bed and access to a kitchen, were particularly squalid. Around a quarter of Whitechapel's population lived in lodging houses.

A street in Whitechapel in the 1880s.

There were some attempts to improve housing. George Peabody paid for the building of 11 blocks of flats in a former slum. The Peabody Estate opened in 1881 and tenants were charged reasonable rents.

Provision for the poor

Like elsewhere, workhouses in Whitechapel were seen as the last resort. They offered a bed and food in return for hard labour. Conditions were deliberately poor, families were split up and inmates had to wear a uniform. Most were elderly, ill, disabled, orphans or unmarried mothers.

After 1880, many young orphans were cared for in Barnardo's homes, where conditions were much better than the workhouse.

Lack of employment opportunities

There was high unemployment because of an economic depression, and few jobs were available to women so many turned to prostitution to survive. Those that had jobs:

* worked long hours for low pay in factories in 'sweated' trades, where conditions were cramped and dirty
* worked building the railways or in the dockyards. Pay was better but numbers required were variable so weekly incomes varied enormously.

All these factors led to high levels of poverty and deprivation in the area.

The link between the environment and crime

The significance of Whitechapel as an inner-city area of poverty, discontent and crime is due to:

* low income levels that led to stealing for survival by those desperate to avoid the workhouse
* unreliable (or lack of) work that meant many had a lot of 'spare' time, which led to alcoholism, disruptive behaviour and violence

* overcrowding that led to tensions between residents (especially between London-born and Irish and Jewish immigrants), which often spilt over into violence
* the high levels of prostitution that led to violence on women.

Tensions between native-born Londoners and immigrants are explored on page 27.

Turn to page 28 for more about different types of crime and the difficulties in policing them. For more about some of the worst cases of violence against women, see page 29.

Now try this

Give reasons why (a) theft and (b) assault were very common crimes in Whitechapel c1870–c1900.

Tensions in Whitechapel

Whitechapel was a melting pot of different people, religions and revolutionary groups. Its population included many temporary residents and immigrants from Ireland and Eastern Europe.

Irish immigrants

- Many Irish left Ireland for the USA in the 1840s but ended up in London instead.
- Poverty meant most could only afford to live in the least expensive parts of London.
- Most worked as navvies (labourers building roads, railways or canals) or dockers.
- They had a reputation for being drunk and violent and were also associated with terrorism, such as the Fenians, who were seen as fanatical terrorists fighting for Ireland's independence from Britain.

An illustration of Wentworth Street, Whitechapel.

Fluctuating population

- Most accommodation in Whitechapel was temporary, which meant there were many temporary residents who didn't have an interest in fostering any sense of community.

Eastern European immigrants

- Huge influx of Eastern European immigrants into Whitechapel in the 1880s who were mostly Russian and Polish Jews, and who had fled persecution in the Russian Empire after Tsar Alexander II's assassination in 1881.
- Poverty meant they were only able to settle in the cheaper parts of London.
- Tended to stick together within these areas, causing segregation. By 1888, some parts of Whitechapel had a 95% Jewish population.

Anarchists and socialists

- From 1848 there was a wave of attempted revolutions across Europe. Many of the revolutionaries ended up in London's East End.
- Movements set up or supported by the revolutionaries were anarchism, which opposed organised government, and socialism, which wanted the end of capitalism.
- Both movements were feared by the authorities, and middle and upper classes, but attracted some support from residents of Whitechapel.

Resulting tensions

As a result of its varied and fluctuating population, tensions in Whitechapel were high.

- There were tensions between immigrant and local populations over access to housing and jobs.
- Recently arrived Jewish immigrants were prepared to accept lower pay and poor conditions, leading to an increase in the sweatshop system – this annoyed other workers and non-sweatshop employers.

- Anti-Semitism and violence against Jews rose rapidly.
- Anyone with a foreign accent was suspected of being a violent revolutionary.
- 'Foreigners' were blamed for many crimes, such as the Ripper murders, which increased racial hatred and violence.

Now try this

Give at least **three** reasons why Irish and Eastern European Jewish immigrants were feared by the other residents of Whitechapel.

The organisation of policing in Whitechapel

The Metropolitan Police Force was divided up into divisions. Whitechapel was under the jurisdiction of H Division. There were many difficulties in policing the area.

The work of H Division

H Division beat constables were each given a set route within Whitechapel to patrol. They were on the look-out for trouble and stopped and questioned people to find out what they were doing. They regularly had to report to their sergeant and everything was recorded in a diary.

Attitudes to the police

All policing in Whitechapel was made more difficult by most of the locals' attitudes. The police was mistrusted, generally, and was seen as part of the government that didn't care for working-class people. This meant that few cooperated with investigations. Police constables were frequently attacked.

See page 26 for more on the environment of Whitechapel and page 27 for more on racial tensions.

The environment
Dark, narrow alleys and courts with multiple doorways into rookeries packed with people and their possessions made chasing and finding criminals extremely difficult.

Gangs
Alongside individual petty thieves, large professional gangs of thieves and pickpockets operated. They 'employed' individuals who were well-trained at both stealing and getting away from the crime.

Violent demonstrations
Public protests were fairly common in Whitechapel. The Social Democratic Federation was involved in many of these protests, such as the Trafalgar Square demonstration in November 1887. Large numbers of angry people in one place frequently, led to disorder and violence and needed a large number of police to deal with them.

Prostitution
With very few jobs available to women, some turned to prostitution to survive. By 1888, approximately 1200 prostitutes, vulnerable to violence, worked in brothels or on the streets.

Problems in policing Whitechapel for H Division

Alcohol
The large number of pubs and gin houses in Whitechapel sold very strong alcohol at affordable prices. Drunkenness frequently fuelled violence. Many alcoholics turned to crime to feed their habit.

Protection rackets
Gangs, such as the Bessarabians, demanded 'protection money' to 'protect' people's businesses. Refusal led to property damage and violence. Fear of these gangs meant people very rarely reported them to the police and either paid up or retaliated with violence themselves.

Attacks on Jews
After large-scale Jewish immigration in the 1880s, attacks on Jews became common. Some police were anti-Semitic themselves, while the language barrier prevented others from helping catch their attackers.

The Whitechapel Vigilance Committee, 1888

 Set up by businessmen in Whitechapel on 10 September, due to the police's lack of progress in catching the 'Ripper' murderer.

 Offered a reward for information leading to the capture of the murderer.

 Patrolled the streets every night with torches (burning wood) and whistles.

☑ Disrupted the police investigation, but also hampered the police by sending false leads and encouraging criticism of the police in newspapers.

Now try this

List **three** factors that made catching criminals in Whitechapel difficult for the police.

Investigative policing in Whitechapel

The Met developed new methods of detective investigation that were to prove useful in investigating the crimes of Jack the Ripper, who murdered at least five women in and around Whitechapel in the autumn of 1888.

Investigative policing techniques

- House-to-house searches for evidence.
  In the Ripper case the pubs and opium dens were searched.

- Distributing leaflets and advertising in newspapers appealing for information from the public.
  In the Ripper case 80000 leaflets were distributed.

- Following up clues found or not found at the crime scenes.
  In the Ripper case it was noted that one of the victim's rings had been taken.

- Following up evidence from the bodies detailed by post mortems and coroners' reports.
  In the Ripper case the police visited hospitals, as some of the mutilated bodies were thought to show the murderer had good knowledge of anatomy.

- Detailed annotated sketches of the crime scenes were drawn and photographs taken.
  In the Ripper case these were used to compare murders with others.

- Setting up soup kitchens to encourage the poorest to come forward with information.

- Interviewing witnesses or suspects including those provided by tip-offs.

Improvements after 1888

 The Met introduced the Bertillon system of taking measurements and photographs of suspects and keeping these records centrally so they could be shared.

 By 1900, the introduction of telephones improved the speed of police communications.

Rival police forces and other problems

There was great rivalry between the Met and City of London police forces. Rather than share information and cooperate on cases, each force wanted to solve crimes before the other did. Whitechapel overlapped the two police districts so this was a particular problem during the Ripper investigation. There was also conflict between the CID and other parts of the Met. H Division had to continue its usual work as well as help CID investigate the murders.

The media

This caused problems for the police as, although media coverage encouraged the public to come forward, it also attracted hoax letters and thousands of theories on the identity of the killer, all of which had to be investigated. Media coverage also stirred up racial hatred, as the media was convinced that an 'Englishman' could not have committed such awful crimes. This led to more violence for the police to deal with, as attacks and discrimination against foreigners increased. The media also added to the pressure on the police by criticising the investigation.

Lurid reports and illustrations of the murders appeared in the media.

Jack the Ripper

Between 31 August and 9 November 1888, five women were strangled and mutilated in Whitechapel. The murderer became known as Jack the Ripper because this was the name used on some letters sent to the police. To this day the murderer has never been discovered, though there are hundreds of theories about who it was.

Now try this

Give **one** way in which the media (a) helped and (b) hindered the police investigation into the Whitechapel murders.

Exam overview

This page introduces you to the main features and requirements of the Paper 1 Option 10 exam paper.

About Paper 1

- Paper 1 is for both your thematic study (Section B) and your study of a historic environment (Section A).
- Section A will be on Whitechapel, c1870–c1900: crime, policing and the inner city.
- Section B will be on Crime and punishment in Britain, c1000–present.
- You will receive two documents: a question paper, which you write into, and a sources booklet, which you will need for some questions in Section A.

The Paper 1 exam lasts for 1 hour 15 minutes (75 minutes) in total. You should spend about 25 minutes on the historic environment and 50 minutes on the thematic study.

You can see examples of all questions on pages 31–38, and in the practice questions on pages 39–56.

The questions

The questions for Paper 1 will always follow this pattern.

Section A: Question 1

Describe **two** features of …   **(4 marks)**

Question 1 targets AO1. AO1 is about showing your **knowledge** and **understanding** of key features and characteristics of the topic.

Section A: Question 2(a)

How useful are Sources A and B for an enquiry into …?

Explain your answer, using Sources A and B and your knowledge of the historical context. **(8 marks)**

Question 2(a) targets AO3, which is about analysing, evaluating and using sources to make substantiated judgements. This is where you show your ability to **analyse** and **evaluate** the usefulness of **sources**.

Section A: Question 2(b)

How could you follow up Source [A/B] to find out more about …?   **(4 marks)**

Complete the table, giving the question you would ask and the type of source you could use.

Question 2(b) also targets AO3. This is where you show your ability to use **sources** to frame historical questions.

Section B: Question 3

Explain **one** way in which … was similar to/different from …   **(4 marks)**

Question 3 targets both AO1 and AO2. AO2 is about explaining and analysing key events using historical concepts, such as causation, consequence, change, continuity, similarity and difference. This question focuses on **similarity** and **difference** across two periods of time.

Section B: Question 4

Explain why …   **(12 marks)**

Two prompts and your own information.

Question 4 also targets both AO1 and AO2. It focuses on causation: explaining why something happened.

Section B: Question 5 or 6

'Statement' and How far do you agree?

Explain your answer.

    (16 marks plus 4 marks for SPaG and use of specialist terminology)

Two prompts and your own information.

You have to answer either Question 5 or Question 6. These target both AO1 and AO2 and you need to make a **judgement** in each question. Up to 4 marks are available for spelling, punctuation, grammar (SPaG) and use of specialist terminology.

Question 1: Describing features

Question 1 on your exam paper will ask you to 'Describe **two** features of ...'. There are four marks available for this question: two for each feature you describe.

Worked example

Describe **two** features of the Whitechapel workhouses.   **(4 marks)**

What does 'describe' mean?

Describe means to give an account of the main characteristics of something. You develop your description with relevant details, but you do not need to include reasons or justifications.

Links You can revise workhouses on page 26.

Sample answer

Feature 1

There were many workhouses in Whitechapel. They were there to support the poorest in society who had no other means of supporting themselves.

Make sure you read the question – it's asking for features of the workhouses, not reasons why they were there.

Feature 2

Conditions in the workhouses in Whitechapel were deliberately poor to put people off going unless they had no choice.

This is a feature but it needs more development and detail describing the conditions.

Improved answer

Feature 1

Conditions in the workhouses in Whitechapel were deliberately poor to put people off going unless they had no choice. The food supplied was very basic and the beds were simple with very basic bed linen.

This improves Feature 2 from above by adding in more detail about the 'poor' conditions.

Feature 2

All beds were in dormitories. There were separate dormitories for men, women and children, so married couples and families were split up.

You need to describe two separate features as done here. Feature 2 describes a completely separate feature of the workhouses to Feature 1.

Source skills 1

In your exam, Questions 2(a) and 2(b) are based on **sources**. Question 2(a) will ask you about the **usefulness** of the sources and Question 2(b) will ask you how you would **follow up information** in one source.

Usefulness

1 Content

- What information in the sources is relevant to the enquiry?
- How useful is this information?

Underline and annotate information in the source to help you with this.

2 Provenance

- Nature: the type of source it is.
- Origins: who produced it and when.
- Purpose: the reason the source was created.
- How do these things impact on the usefulness of the source?

Remember that this isn't necessarily about the amount of information given. A small piece of information can be very useful!

Remember that an unreliable source can still be useful.

3 Context

- Use your own knowledge of the enquiry topic to evaluate the source.
- Is the information in the source accurate compared with what you know?

Remember to think about what information is missing from the source as well as what's included.

Following up sources

For Question 2(b) you have to complete a table like the one below.

Detail in Source X that I would follow up:

....

Question I would ask:

....

What type of source I could use:

....

How this might help answer my question:

....

This has to be related to the enquiry given in the question.

This must be related to the enquiry and the detail you've written above.

There are likely to be many different types of sources, but make sure you choose one that will really help investigate the question you've written above.

You should write one or two sentences explaining how the type of source chosen above could help you answer your question.

Examples of sources: national

- National government statistics.
- National newspaper articles and reports.
- National police records.

Examples of sources: local

- Personal accounts by police officers, victims and witnesses.
- Photographs.
- Police records from H Division.
- Court records and freedom licences.

Source skills 2

In your exam you will be given a source booklet containing two sources. Both Questions 2(a) and 2(b) require you to **analyse** the sources so it is important that you spend time reading and looking at these sources carefully before you start your answers. You could also annotate the sources to help you.

Source A: An illustration of Wentworth Street, Whitechapel, drawn in 1872. The illustration appeared in *London: A Pilgrimage*, a book of illustrations by Gustave Doré.

Take notice of any dates given. Does this tie in with what you know about the housing at this time?

It's vital to read the information given about each source as this is where you'll find information on the **provenance** (nature, origin and purpose) of that source.

Image sources need analysing as well as text ones! What can you see in the image? What can't you see? How useful is this to the enquiry?

The purpose of illustrations can be difficult to assess as it is often not known why they were drawn.

To what extent can you trust this person to give information relevant to your enquiry? This will affect how useful any information given is.

Source B: A description of the inside of a lodging house by Hugh Edward Hoare which first appeared in the *National Review* and later in the *Cambridge Independent Press* on 14 September 1888. Hoare was a wealthy philanthropist who took over the running of a lodging house in Whitechapel in 1886 and later became an MP.

Two dates are given. How does this account compare with what you know about lodging houses around this time?

When you're reading the source, highlight any particularly useful information it gives that is relevant to the enquiry.

Passing the outer door, we found ourselves opposite a little window in a recess, where the "deputy", or manager, sits to collect the four pence for the night's lodging, and where he keeps the food which he sells to the lodgers. Passing through the second door, we enter a moderate-sized low "kitchen", where about twenty men and women were sitting on long wooden benches, or standing round the fire. … Plain long deal tables and benches were set round the room. On the chimney-piece were several tin teapots, and in a cupboard the coarse plates and cups and saucers for the free use of the lodgers ... Underground was the washing-place and coke cellar, on the first floor were the beds for the couples, and above that a large dormitory for single men, containing sixteen beds.

Question 2(a): Usefulness of sources

Question 2(a) on your exam paper will ask you how useful two sources are for a particular enquiry. There are eight marks available for this question.

Worked example

Study Sources A and B on page 33.

How useful are Sources A and B for an enquiry into the nature of housing in Whitechapel between 1870 and 1900?

Explain your answer, using Sources A and B and your knowledge of the historical context.

(8 marks)

Sample extract

Source A is an illustration of Whitechapel slums drawn in 1872. It is fairly useful as it gives a good idea of the nature of some housing. The building looks in poor condition and there are many people in the drawing, indicating that the house is very overcrowded. The people and their clothes look dirty, indicating that there were poor washing facilities, if any, available. However, we cannot tell how wide or typical these conditions were as only a small part of Whitechapel is shown.

The caption tells us that this was drawn in 1872 and I know that there was a lot of slum housing in some parts of Whitechapel at this time. Slum areas were known as rookeries and houses were very tightly packed in these areas with no gardens or green space. Houses were indeed very overcrowded with whole families living in just one room and sanitation was poor.

It's difficult to know why this source was created but it may well have been to indicate the poor conditions that people lived in at the time. Therefore, the artist may have exaggerated conditions or chosen to depict the worst of it. This means that the source may not be totally reliable.

Source B is written by someone who ran a lodging house …

What does 'how useful' mean?

How useful means how valuable are the sources for a specific enquiry. You need to come to a judgement on how useful each of the sources is for the enquiry given in the question.

Links You can revise housing in Whitechapel on page 26.

Always make a **judgement** on how useful a source is and then explain why you have reached this decision. This answer has done this by saying the source is fairly useful because it shows housing conditions.

With image sources, always give a brief description of what you can see that is relevant to the enquiry as the student has done here.

Use your **own knowledge** of the topic to analyse the source – this student tells us that they know that housing in some parts of Whitechapel was very poor at this time.

Remember to only include information that is directly relevant to the source, which this student does.

Remember to include reasons why the source was created. For images this can be quite tricky as we often don't know but the student has tried to do this and successfully links this to the possible unreliability of the source.

You **must** use both sources in your answer so it's good to see that this student is continuing their answer by looking at Source B.

Question 2(b): Following up sources

Question 2(b) on your exam paper will ask you to pick a detail from one source and explain how you would follow up that detail in another source. There are four marks available for this question.

Worked example

Study Source B on page 33.

How could you follow up Source B to find out more about the nature of housing in Whitechapel between 1870 and 1900?

In your answer, you must give the question you would ask and the type of source you could use.

Complete the table below.   **(4 marks)**

Detail in Source B that I would follow up: '...four pence for the night's lodging.'
Question I would ask: How affordable was four pence for a night's   lodging at this time?
What type of source I could use: An employer's account.
How this might help answer my question: This would help see how much money four   pence would leave for other essentials like   food.

What does 'follow up' mean?

Follow up means investigate something further. In other words, how you could find out more information on something in one source using another source.

🔗 **Links**   You can revise housing in Whitechapel on page 26.

The table is provided to help you structure your answer so make sure you use the prompts as the student has done here.

Make sure the question is linked to the detail you have used in the first part of your answer.

Remember, you only need to give one type of source here. There is only one mark for each of the points so don't waste time going into more detail than is necessary.

This answer must relate to the type of source and the enquiry question you have chosen.

Question 3: Making comparisons

Question 3 on your exam paper will ask you to explain **one** way in which something was similar or different over time. There are four marks available for this question.

🔗 **Links** You can revise medieval punishments on page 5, and 19th century punishments on page 16.

What does 'explain one way' mean?

Explain one way means providing details of one way in which something was similar or different over time. You do not need to explain the reasons for the similarity or difference.

Worked example

Explain **one** way in which Norman punishments for crimes against property were different to punishments for crimes against property in the 19th century.

(4 marks)

Sample answer

Norman punishments were very harsh and were carried out in public. This was seen as the best way to deter crime and enforce Norman law. The death penalty was often given for crimes against property, such as theft. Other punishments included castration, blinding and amputating limbs.

In the early 19th century, punishments for crimes against property were similar as many offences were punished by death, usually hanging, until the end of the Bloody Code in the 1820s. After 1825 they were different because few people received a death sentence. Punishment for theft was often transportation to Australia until it was abolished in 1868. Then prisons were used instead.

 Don't give a general description of punishments as the student has done here! You have to give details of how punishments for crimes against property were different.

 Make sure you answer the question asked. The question is about how punishments were different – this answer mentions punishment by death for crimes against property being the same in the Norman and 19th century periods which is not what is required.

 The question asks for 'one' way so only one is needed. There is no need to give more than one.

Improved answer

Norman punishments for crimes against property were very harsh. The death penalty, usually by hanging, was often given for crimes such as theft.

In the 19th century, punishments for crimes against property were different from the 1820s because fewer people received a death sentence. Punishment for theft was often transportation to Australia until this was abolished in 1868.

 Make sure you just give **one** way as the student has done here and focus on difference, not similarities.

 This question is only worth four marks so long answers are not required. Spending too long on this question will mean you run out of time for the ones worth more marks.

 You need to give some detail of how punishments for crimes against property were different – focusing on just one way.

Question 4: Explaining why

Question 4 on your exam paper is about causation: **explaining why** something happened. There are 12 marks available for this question and two prompts to help you answer; you must also use information of your own.

Worked example

Explain why there were changes in punishments for witchcraft in the period c1600–c1750.

You may use the following in your answer:

- Matthew Hopkins
- The Royal Society

You **must** also use information of your own.

(12 marks)

Sample extract

The crime of witchcraft was regarded as a very serious crime in 1600. It could therefore be punished with the death penalty. By 1750, however, it had stopped being a crime altogether. The Witchcraft Act of 1736 repealed the witchcraft laws. From then on people who claimed to use magic could be fined or put in prison.

Matthew Hopkins was known as the Witchfinder General. He was employed to find witches in Essex and East Anglia during the English Civil War. He helped to stir up mass panic and fear of witches during 1645–47. This was a period of witch-hunts when an unprecedented number of people were convicted and hanged for the crime of witchcraft.

Improved extract

Fear and hatred of witches in the first half of the 17th century was exploited by people such as Matthew Hopkins, known as the Witchfinder General. He was employed to find witches in Essex and East Anglia during the English Civil War and helped to stir up mass panic and fear of witches during 1645–47. This was a period of witch-hunts when an unprecedented number of people were convicted and hanged for the crime of witchcraft. The punishment was so harsh as it was feared so much at this time. This contrasts with later periods when far fewer people were hanged because fear of witches had declined.

What does 'explain why' mean?

Explain why means saying how or why something happened, backed up with examples or justifications to support the reasons you give. Good ways to get into an explanation are to use sentence starters like 'One reason for this was ...' or 'This was because ...'

Links You can revise witchcraft on pages 12 and 14.

It's a good idea to start your answer, as here, with a summary of what changed. Ideally, though, you would also offer a brief explanation of why this change happened, which you would develop through the rest of your answer.

You can use the prompts given in the question to help you but you must use the prompt to explain why changes happened. This second paragraph follows one of the prompts and demonstrates good factual knowledge (AO1) of Matthew Hopkins' work in Essex and East Anglia, but does not use this knowledge to explain why (AO2) witchcraft was harshly punished at this time.

You must link your own knowledge with explanation and you must also **use some of your own knowledge** and not just rely on the bullets provided.

The best answers will link knowledge with an explanation of change. Crucially here, this answer begins to explain the link between the great fear of witches and work of Matthew Hopkins to the harsh punishment for witchcraft during the English Civil War period.

The answer needs to continue by explaining how attitudes towards witchcraft changed which led to a decrease in the harshness of punishment for the crime.

Question 5/6: Making a judgement

Question 5/6 on your exam paper involves **analysing the statement** in the question and deciding how far you agree with it. There are 16 marks available (20 marks in total when SPaG is included) for this question and two prompts to help you; you must also use information of your own.

Worked example

'The setting up of the Metropolitan Police Force was the most important development in law enforcement during the period c1700–c1900.'

How far do you agree? Explain your answer.

You may use the following in your answer:

- The work of the Fielding brothers
- The 1856 Police Act

You **must** also use information of your own.

(16 marks plus 4 marks for SPaG and use of specialist terminology)

Sample extract

Although the setting up of the Metropolitan Police Force was an important development in law enforcement between 1700 and 1900, I disagree that it was the most important development.

The work of the Fielding brothers was another very important development in law enforcement at this time. Henry Fielding was Chief Magistrate at Bow Street Court and he set up and ran the Bow Street Runners in 1749 to try to tackle the huge rise in crime rates in London since 1700. He was succeeded by his half-brother, John. The Bow Street Runners tried both to detect crime by employing people to find evidence and track down criminals and to prevent crime by employing people to patrol major roads on foot and horse. This was an important precedent for the Metropolitan Police. The Bow Street Runners was the first truly 'professional' force as runners were paid for their work, firstly through private fees and rewards and, after 1785, through government funding. They were also fairly successful on the detecting side and brought many criminals to justice. There were too few patrols to really have an impact on reducing the crime rate. However ...

Analysing the statement

The statement will always give a judgement on something. You decide whether you agree or not by weighing up points that support the statement with points that oppose it.

SPaG

In your answer to this question you will receive up to four marks for your spelling, punctuation and grammar and your use of specialist terms so check your work carefully. Remember to use as much specialist terminology as you can.

Links You can revise law enforcement c1700–c1900 on page 15.

Remember to give a clear indication whether you agree or disagree with the quotation. It doesn't matter whether you agree or not but you **must** state your opinion and then back it up.

Add in your own knowledge where you can. This answer demonstrates some good own knowledge of the Bow Street Runners.

This part of the answer concentrates on points that disagree with the statement, but it's important to look at points that agree with the statement, too. In this case, the student should continue their answer by writing in detail about the setting up of the Metropolitan Police.

Practice

Put your skills and knowledge into practice with the following question.

> **Option 10: Crime and punishment in Britain, c1000–present**
> *and* **Whitechapel, c1870–c1900: crime, policing and the inner city**

SECTION A: Whitechapel, c1870–c1900: crime, policing and the inner city

Answer Questions 1 and 2.

1 Describe **two** features of the work of a 'beat' constable c1870–c1900.

(4 marks)

Feature 1

Guided   The 'beat' was a set route around streets

....

....

....

....

....

Feature 2

....

....

....

....

....

....

You have to answer all questions in Section A. You should spend about 25 minutes on this section. Remember to leave five minutes or so to check your work when you've finished writing.

 Links You can revise the work of the police on page 25.

 You need to identify **two** valid features and support each feature.

 Your exam paper will have a separate space for each feature you need to describe.

 Describe means you have to give an account of the main characteristic. You do not need to explain why the feature was important or what it was trying to achieve.

Practice

Put your skills and knowledge into practice with the following question.

2 (a) Study Sources A and B on page 56.

How useful are Sources A and B for an enquiry into the problems encountered by the police investigating the Whitechapel murders?

Explain your answer, using Sources A and B and your knowledge of the historical context.   **(8 marks)**

....
....
....
....
....
....
....
....
....
....
....
....
....
....
....
....
....
....
....
....
....
....
....
....
....

Spend some time studying and annotating the sources after you have read the question.

Links You can revise the policing of the Whitechapel murders on page 29.

Make sure you use **both** sources in your answer and come to a judgement about how useful each source is.

You should give the strengths and weaknesses of each source for this particular enquiry – problems encountered by the police investigating the Whitechapel murders.

Remember the key things to include for each source: content, provenance and your own knowledge.

See page 32 for more information on content and provenance.

For instance, you might describe Source A as being useful as an example of media criticism of the police and the fact that it directs the police towards a suspect, based only on the fact that they think he is unpleasant and Jewish.

Practice

Use this page to continue your answer to question 2(a).

....

....

....

⬅ It's a good idea to conclude your answer by again stating how useful you think both sources are.

....

....

....

⬅ Remember, you don't need to compare the sources!

....

....

....

....

....

....

....

....

....

....

....

....

....

....

....

....

....

....

....

....

....

....

Practice

Put your skills and knowledge into practice with the following question.

2 (b) Study Source B on page 56.

How could you follow up Source B to find out more about the problems encountered by the police investigating the Whitechapel murders?

In your answer, you must give the question you would ask and the type of source you could use.

Complete the table below.   **(4 marks)**

Detail in Source B that I would follow up:

....

....

....

Question I would ask:

....

....

....

What type of source I could use:

....

....

....

How this might help answer my question:

....

....

....

....

Links You can revise the policing of the Whitechapel murders on page 29.

You will be given a table with writing lines, which you should write your answer into. There are only four marks for this question so you don't need to spend time going into detail.

It's important that you focus on the enquiry given in the question here – there are several details in the source that you may like to follow up, but it has to be relevant to problems encountered by the police investigating the Whitechapel murders.

This question must relate to the detail you've given above.

There are many sources that you could suggest here, but you need to be able to say how your chosen source might help to answer your question. So make sure you pick a source you will be able to explain clearly.

See page 32 for types of sources you could suggest.

Practice

Put your skills and knowledge into practice with the following question.

SECTION B: Crime and punishment in Britain, c1000–present
Answer Questions 3 and 4. Then answer EITHER Question 5 OR 6.

3 Explain **one** way in which the purposes of punishments for crimes were different in the 18th and 20th centuries.

(4 marks)

....

....

....

....

....

....

....

....

....

....

....

🔗 **Links** You can revise punishments in the 18th century on page 16 and in the 20th century on page 22.

Remember just to give **one** way as the question asks. For example, you could focus on rehabilitation by saying how this was a major purpose of punishment in the 20th century but wasn't really considered in the 18th century.

You don't need to explain why they were different – just how! The question is only worth four marks and there's limited writing space so don't waste too much time on answering this question.

Practice

Put your skills and knowledge into practice with the following question.

4 Explain why there were changes in the number of capital crimes in the period 1800–2000.

You may use the following in your answer:
- The Bloody Code
- Derek Bentley

You **must** also use information of your own.   **(12 marks)**

Remember that Question 4 is all about **causation**: this means you are looking for relevant reasons.

Guided The period 1800 to 2000 saw a reduction in the number of offences which carried the death penalty. At the beginning of the 19th century, the number of capital crimes hit a peak of 222. By the end of the 20th century, capital punishment had been completely abolished. This was due to several reasons, such as changing views on the aims of punishment, making punishments more proportionate to the crime, and several controversial cases where capital punishment had been used against many people's wishes.

For example, you might use the first prompt and write about the Bloody Code, which saw the number of capital crimes peak at 222 in 1810 before being substantially reduced in the 1820s.

Links You can revise the use of the death penalty on pages 16, 22 and 24.

In 1800, the vast majority of people believed that the aim of punishment should be retribution and deterrence. It was thought that the death penalty would be the ultimate deterrent. Therefore, as the crime rate was rising dramatically, the number of capital crimes punished increased in an attempt to make people think twice about committing crime. This was the Bloody Code where more offences carried the death penalty. This reached a peak of 222 capital crimes in 1810.

There are 12 marks in total for this question. You don't have to use the prompts in the question in your answer but you **must** include your own information to answer the question fully.

You need to give more than one reason, and the best answers will show how different factors combined to prevent or bring about change.

Your explanations need to stay focused on answering the question. Although you might remember lots of detail, you need to focus on providing **reasons why**, not descriptions of.

Practice

Use this page to continue your answer to question 4.

....

....

....

....

....

....

....

....

....

....

....

....

....

....

....

....

....

....

....

....

....

....

....

....

....

....

Other detail you could include would be the increase in availability of other forms of punishment, especially imprisonment. You could also give detail on the controversial cases of the 1950s: Timothy Evans, Derek Bentley and Ruth Ellis.

Remember, the best answers to question 4 will show a good knowledge of the key features and characteristics of the period, analyse the reasons for change or continuity **and** show how factors combined to bring about change or keep things the same.

Make sure you support your explanation with a good range of accurate and relevant detail throughout your answer.

Practice

Use this page to continue your answer to question 4.

Practice

Put your skills and knowledge into practice with the following question.

Answer EITHER Question 5 OR Question 6.

Spelling, punctuation, grammar and use of specialist terminology will be assessed in this question.

EITHER

5 'William I's Forest Laws were the most significant changes to crime after the Norman Conquest.'
How far do you agree? Explain your answer.

(16 marks, plus 4 marks for SPaG)

You may use the following in your answer:
• Murdrum fine
• Church courts
You **must** also use information of your own.

OR

6 'Law enforcement was the responsibility of communities between c1300 and c1700'.
How far do you agree? Explain your answer.

(16 marks, plus 4 marks for SPaG)

You may use the following in your answer:
• the hue and cry system
• Justices of the Peace Act, 1361
You **must** also use information of your own.

You have a choice of two questions for your final question of the exam. Each question is worth the same number of marks. Although one might immediately seem a question you can answer, do read both carefully to check your choice is the right one.

On the exam paper, Questions 5 and 6 will be on one page, and you will then turn to the next page to write your answer – like the layout here.

 You can revise the Forest Laws on page 2 and law enforcement c1300–c1700 on pages 4 and 9.

Total for Question 5 = 20 marks. There are 16 marks plus four marks for spelling, punctuation, grammar and use of specialist terminology.

If you decide to answer Question 5 turn to page 48. If you decide to answer Question 6, turn to page 52.

Choosing a question

At the top of the first answer page there will be an instruction for you to indicate which of the two questions you have chosen to answer. You do this by making a cross in the box for Question 5 or Question 6.

Don't worry if you put a cross in the wrong box by mistake. Just put a line through the cross and then put a new cross in the right box.

Practice

Use this page to begin your answer to question 5.

Indicate which question you are answering by marking a cross in the box. If you change your mind, put a line through the box and then indicate your new question with a cross.

Chosen question number: **Question 5** ☒ **Question 6** ☐

Guided I agree that William I's Forest Laws were the most significant changes to crime after the Norman Conquest. This is because these laws were very harsh and made many actions crimes that had previously been allowed. They also affected many people as about 30% of England was designated Royal Forest.

Remember **only** to answer **either** Question 5 **or** Question 6 in the exam.

As with Question 4, you do not have to use both or either of the two prompts provided by the question. If you do use them, remember that you **must** also include information of your own.

Plan your answer before you start writing. List factors that support the statement in the question and list other factors that go against the statement.

For example:

Support	Against
About 30% of the country became 'Royal Forests', so many people were affected.	William I encouraged churches to set up courts which made some moral actions crimes – affected most of the population.
The Forest Laws were deeply resented and caused great hardship for some people.	The Murdrum fine made murdering a Norman a worse crime than murdering anyone else.

Practice

Use this page to continue your answer to question 5.

....
....
....
....
....
....
....
....
....
....
....
....
....
....
....
....
....
....
....
....
....
....
....
....
....

Bring specific facts and details into your answer to show how well you understand the key features and characteristics that are involved in the question.

End your answer by saying **how far** you agree with the question statement and give support for your decision.

Remember, this question is where you will also receive marks for your spelling, punctuation and grammar and use of specialist terms so write and check your work carefully!

Practice

Use this page to continue your answer to question 5.

....

....

....

....

....

....

....

....

....

....

....

....

....

....

....

....

....

....

....

....

....

....

....

....

....

Practice

....

....

....

Practice

Use this page to continue your answer to question 5.

....

....

....

....

....

....

....

....

....

....

....

....

....

....

....

....

....

....

....

....

....

....

....

....

....

Practice

Use this page to start your answer to question 6.

Indicate which question you are answering by marking a cross in the box. If you change your mind, put a line through the box and then indicate your new question with a cross.

Chosen question number: **Question 5** ☐   **Question 6** [x]

> Remember **only** to answer **either** Question 5 **or** Question 6 in the exam.

Guided   I largely agree that law enforcement was the

responsibility of communities between c1300 and c1700.

There was no national police force. Members of the

community were expected to raise and join the hue and

cry, volunteer as constables and members of the night

watch, and witnesses to crime were expected to try to

stop suspected criminals and take them to the authorities.

However, the authorities did become more involved through

appointing officials to act as judges and catch criminals.

....

....

....

....

....

....

....

....

....

....

....

....

....

....

....

....

....

> As with Question 4, you do not have to use both or either of the two prompts provided by the question. If you do use them, remember that you **must** also include information of your own.

> Plan your answer before you start writing. List factors that support the statement in the question and list other factors that go against the statement.

> For example:

Support	Against
The hue and cry system was the main way of catching criminals.	Justices of the Peace were appointed by the king after 1361 to try small crimes.
The hue and cry was led by the parish constable – a male volunteer, appointed by the community.	Sheriffs were government officials whose role included tracking down criminals using a posse of local men.
Members of the night watch were community volunteers who patrolled at night.	Trial by ordeal and by combat had been abolished.

Practice

Use this page to continue your answer to question 6.

....
....
....
....
....
....
....
....
....
....
....
....
....
....
....
....
....
....
....
....
....
....
....
....
....
....
....
....

Bring specific facts and details into your answer to show how well you understand the key features and characteristics that are involved in the question.

End your answer by saying **how far** you agree with the question statement and give support for your decision.

Remember, this question is where you will also receive marks for your spelling, punctuation and grammar and use of specialist terms so write and check your work carefully!

Practice

Use this page to continue your answer to question 6.

Practice

Use this page to continue your answer to question 6.

....

....

....

....

....

....

....

....

....

....

....

....

....

....

....

....

....

....

....

....

....

....

....

....

....

Sources Booklet

Use these sources to answer the questions in Section A (see pages 40–42).

Sources for use with Section A.

Source A: From *The Star* newspaper on 5 September 1888, five days after the murder of Mary Ann Nichols, the first victim of the criminal who became known as Jack the Ripper.

> Whitechapel is loud in its indignation over the efficiency of the detectives and is asking several questions to which there does not seem to be any satisfactory answer. Among other things the people wish to know why the police do not arrest "Leather Apron". "Leather Apron" by himself is quite an unpleasant character … he is a more ghoulish and devilish brute than can be found in all the pages of shocking fiction … His name nobody knows, but all are united in the belief that he is a Jew or of Jewish parentage his face being of a marked Hebrew type …

Source B: From *The Daily News*, 13 October 1888, several weeks after the Whitechapel Vigilance Committee offered a reward for information leading to the capture of the Whitechapel murderer.

> A corps of detectives had in their possession quite a bulky packet of papers all relating to information supplied to the police, and all, as a detective remarked, "amounting to nothing".
>
> "The difficulty of our work," he said, "is much greater than the general public are aware of. The reward for the apprehension of the murderer has had one effect – it has inundated us with descriptions of persons into whose movements we are expected to inquire for the sole reason that they have of late been noticed to keep rather irregular hours and to take their meals alone.
> Some of these cases we have sent men to investigate, and the persons who it has proved have been unjustly suspected have been very indignant, and naturally so.
>
> We do not expect that the batch of inquiries to be undertaken today will lead to any more satisfactory result than those of previous days …"

Answers

Where an exemplar answer is given, this is not necessarily the only correct response. In most cases there is a range of responses that can gain full marks.

SUBJECT CONTENT

Crime and punishment in Britain, c1000–present

c1000–c1500: Medieval England

1. Crime in Medieval England

(a) Crimes against the person – crimes that cause physical harm to person, e.g. murder, assault.

(b) Crimes against property – crimes where another person's property is taken or damaged, e.g. theft, arson.

(c) Crimes against authority – crimes that threaten leaders of a country or the country itself, e.g. treason, terrorism.

2. 'New' crimes in Norman England

Any three from:

- Many had been evicted from their homes or farms to make way for the Royal Forests.
- Activities that had previously been allowed, such as killing rabbits and collecting firewood, were now illegal. At best, this irritated ordinary people; at worst, it made the everyday struggle for survival harder.
- Punishments for breaking the Forest Laws were extremely harsh.
- The foresters who enforced the Forest Laws were often violent.

3. Anglo-Saxon law enforcement

Reasons include:

- It was effective, so there wasn't a need for anything else.
- People felt a strong sense of duty towards their community; the vast majority of people lived in very small communities, so it was easy to enforce the law in this way.
- There weren't any other options.

4. Norman and later medieval law enforcement

Differences include (any two from):

- Parish constables were appointed to help keep the peace, arrest people and lead the chase after the hue and cry.
- Knights were appointed to keep the peace, which evolved into JPs who acted as judges in small courts.
- Posses were formed to help sheriffs chase and catch criminals.
- Trial by ordeal and by combat was abolished in 1215.

5. Medieval punishments

Any three from:

- All used capital punishments.
- All used corporal punishments.
- All used fines.
- All punished people differently depending on social class, gender, etc.
- Crimes against authority were punished the harshest across all three.
- The aims of punishment were the same across the periods.

6. The influence of the Church

Any three from:

- Church courts tried people for different crimes to other courts – moral crimes.
- Church courts tried people for not following Church rites, such as attending Mass regularly.
- Church courts tried priests for all crimes (priests wouldn't be tried in any other court).
- Church courts dispensed more lenient punishment than other courts to give criminals a chance to repent and reform.

c1500–c1700: Early modern England

7. Crime in early modern England

There were more charges of treason as there were many rebellions against the monarch. When the monarch became head of the Church (after 1534, except for Mary I), anyone challenging the Church was therefore committing an act of treason.

There were more charges of heresy because the official religion of the country kept changing from Catholic to Protestant and Protestant to Catholic. Some Protestants were executed for heresy throughout this period, however Catholics were more likely to be executed for treason.

8. 'New' crimes in early modern England

Any three from:

- Vagrants were commonly viewed as lazy and responsible for their own misfortune.
- Some vagrants did turn to theft – many people thought all vagrants were criminals and feared them.
- The big increase in the number of vagrants was itself seen as threatening by 'settled' people.
- Fear of the 'unknown' – most vagrants were unknown in the towns and cities, as they had moved there to find work (during the Middle Ages, everyone in the community was known to everyone else).
- People resented having to pay to support vagrants.

9. Law enforcement in early modern England

Any three from:

- Local people were still expected to raise the hue and cry and join in to catch criminals when a crime took place.
- Witnesses to a crime were expected to stop it and report it to the JP.

- Householders in the area were all expected to serve as night watchmen, who patrolled the local area at night.
- Local people appointed a local person as the constable.

10. Punishment in early modern England

- Retribution – to severely punish the person for committing crime.
- To act as a deterrent to stop others from committing crime.
- To remove criminals from society and therefore protect people (in the case of capital punishment, or prisons for vagabonds).
- Humiliation for criminals in the case of corporal punishment.
- The beginnings of the idea of rehabilitation – giving criminals a chance to repent and change their ways – in the case of transportation.

11. The Gunpowder Plotters, 1605

This was the punishment for treason, which was seen as the worst crime and therefore received the harshest punishment. Punishments for serious crimes at this time were all corporal (physical), so those convicted of treason received the death penalty after enduring extreme pain. The main purpose of punishment at the time was retribution, so this was the ultimate retribution. It was carried out in public to act as a deterrent, to try to prevent others from committing the same crime. Authorities punished serious crime particularly harshly during periods of political and religious instability. The Gunpowder Plot occurred not long after James I has succeeded to the throne, when not all accepted him as king. It was also a time of religious instability. There was widespread fear of Catholicism and Catholic plots to take the throne.

12. The witch-hunts of 1645–47

Any three from:

- The war caused/enhanced economic problems – people looked for scapegoats to blame for their poverty.
- The war brought great social upheaval as many people travelled around the country – 'strangers' were feared.
- The war brought a lack of law and order.
- Individuals stirred up fear of witches.
- Many Puritans were superstitious and believed the Royalists used witchcraft.
- It was usually single women who lived alone who were accused of witchcraft, and the war left more women on their own.

c1700–c1900: 18th and 19th century Britain

13. Crimes against the person and property

Examples of two different attitudes:

- The attitude of the wealthy who considered highwaymen as common robbers, robbing and murdering honest people.
- The attitude of the poor who sometimes saw highwaymen as romantic figures, as reflected in popular ballads about highwaymen.

Reasons for the decline in highway robbery could include any two of:

- Railways reduced the number of stagecoaches in use.
- Being armed and in disguise on a high road was made a capital crime in 1772.
- Mounted police patrols on major roads deterred robbers.

14. Crimes against authority

They were trying to prevent the six men from forming a trade union to protest about their wages. They worried this would lead the men to protest more against their employers and authority figures. More widely, they wanted to deter others from forming trade unions, or taking part in protests against authority figures.

15. Law enforcement

The Fielding brothers established and ran the Bow Street Runners. They were significant because this was the first organised group that aimed to deter crime by both solving crimes, by tracking down criminals and bringing them to justice, and by patrolling streets to deter crime from taking place. They were paid, firstly by victims of crime or people who wanted their streets patrolled, and then, significantly, by the government. They were a more professional force than that previously used.

16. Changing views on the purpose of punishment

Hanging was seen as too harsh for petty crime, so alternatives were looked for. Transportation was used as an alternative, but this began to be seen as too harsh a punishment as well. It was too expensive and Australia didn't want more criminals. There was an increase in prisons, and imprisonment was now seen as an acceptable form of punishment. Some started thinking that punishment should also be about reforming people (shown in Peel's prison reforms).

17. Pentonville Prison

Any three from:

- Cells were equipped with everything a prisoner needed – bed, wash basin, toilet and they were given meals there – so there was no need to mix with other prisoners.
- Items needed for work were also placed in cells, so inmates didn't need to leave the cell.
- Walls were very thick, so prisoners couldn't talk to each other.
- The chapel had individual cubicles, so prisoners couldn't see each other.
- Wings of the prison meant it was impossible to see other prisoners from cell windows.

18. Robert Peel

Any three from:

- The police were now well trained, so knew how to do a good job in preventing and detecting crime.
- Their work was full time and they were well paid, so they wanted to do a good job.
- They won the trust of the general public which helped the police solve crimes.
- Uniformed police patrolling areas of high street crime stopped people from committing crime.

c1900–present: Modern Britain

19. Crime in modern Britain

Any three from:

- 'old' theft – 'new': most forms of cybercrime such as online fraud and identity theft
- 'old' smuggling – 'new': drug-trafficking
- 'old' horse and cart theft – 'new': car theft
- 'old' drunk in charge of a horse – 'new': drink-driving
- 'old' violent attacks using weapons – 'new': terrorist offences using modern weapons.

20. 'New' crimes in modern Britain

(a) Modern transport and high numbers of road users have caused many 'new' crimes (driving offences).

(b) As Britain became more multicultural with people of different races and religions, racism was seen as a crime that should therefore be punished.

21. Law enforcement in modern Britain

Fingerprinting: helps to catch and prosecute criminals, as fingerprints found at the scene can only belong to one person. Databases shared between police forces help to identify people from their fingerprints.

Radios: make it easier for police to report problems and request help if needed.

Computers: used for preventing crime through monitoring electronic communication and used for catching and prosecuting people as police can sort through huge amounts of information in databases.

DNA evidence: like fingerprints, can be used to identify criminals (and victims) from hair, skin or blood found at the scene of a crime.

Cars, motorbikes, helicopters: allow police to get to crime scenes very quickly and chase criminals if necessary.

CCTV: can be used for both prevention (people are deterred from committing crime if they think CCTV is being used) and for identifying and catching criminals once a crime has been committed.

22. Punishment in modern Britain

Any five from:

- Abolition of the death penalty.
- Increasing use of non-custodial sentences; end of hard labour and corporal punishment in prisons.
- Community sentences.
- ASBOs.
- More focus on rehabilitation in prison through education and work.
- Different prisons for different criminals and different people (e.g. women and the young).
- Use of probation.

23. Conscientious objectors

Similarities: COs faced tribunals to decide whether they were genuine; some were given non-combatant roles; some were sent to prison.

Differences: Tribunals during WW2 were not military; far more COs were given complete or partial exemption during WW2; those who were sent to prison during WW2 were not given hard labour or treated as harshly.

24. The Derek Bentley case

- He didn't fire the shot that killed the policeman.
- He had learning difficulties and several doctors gave his mental age as 10.
- The words 'let him have it', which formed part of the case against him, had several interpretations and were not a clear direction for murder.

Whitechapel c1870–c1900: crime, policing and the inner city

The historic environment

25. The Metropolitan Police

At least four from:

- The City of London within London had a separate police force and wasn't policed by the Met.
- Ineffective detective work of the CID.
- Police officers drinking on the job.
- Absenteeism of police officers.
- Lack of numbers compared to the general population.
- Hostile attitudes of some members of the public, especially working classes.

26. The local context of Whitechapel

(a) Theft was very common due to high unemployment, unreliable employment and low wages, which led people to steal for survival; overcrowded conditions meant it was difficult to keep possessions private and stealing them was quite easy; a large number of orphans stole for survival; criminal gangs that operated at a high level.

(b) Assault was very common due to people living at very close quarters; tensions between immigrants and local populations; large numbers of prostitutes meant that assault on women was common; alcohol – large number of pubs, people with spare time, etc.

27. Tensions in Whitechapel

At least three from:

- Different religions (Jewish Eastern Europeans and Catholic Irish) and unfamiliar customs, clothes, food, etc.; 'extreme'/different political views (Irish nationalism/Fenianism, anarchists and socialists).
- Irish immigrants had a reputation for drunkenness and violence.
- Eastern European Jews segregated themselves.
- Different language (Yiddish and, to a far less extent, Gaelic) meant the English didn't know what they were saying and caused mis-communication.
- Many Jews were resented for being successful in business.
- Jewish business owners often preferred employing Jews who would accept lower wages and poorer working conditions.

28. The organisation of policing in Whitechapel

Any three from:

- Distrust and suspicion of the police by locals meant they rarely cooperated; locals greatly feared the gangs and other perpetrators of crime.
- Language barrier – many residents spoke Yiddish, while the police only spoke English.
- Tightly packed housing in alleys made it very easy for criminals to hide and get away.
- Not enough police to deal with the scale and nature of crime in Whitechapel.

29. Investigative policing in Whitechapel

(a) The media coverage encouraged members of the public to go to the police with information; the police actively used the media to ask the public to come forward with information.

(b) The media coverage attracted lots of hoax letters from people pretending to be the killer, which wasted police time; it also attracted thousands of theories on the identity of the killer, which the police wasted time investigating; media coverage and portrayal of the killer as a foreigner stirred up violence and racial hatred.

PRACTICE

39. Practice

1 Any two features from:

- Patrolling a set route around the streets.
- Stopping and questioning people to ask what they're doing.
- Breaking up fights and dealing with trouble they encounter.
- Reporting any incidents to the beat sergeant and recording these in a diary.
- Arresting suspects.

40. Practice

2 (a) Source A: Useful because it's an actual example of media 'interference' and criticism of the police. Questioning why police haven't arrested someone known as 'Leather Apron' but the suspicion of him seems to be just based on people's reporting of his 'unpleasant character'. Also, a good example of anti-Semitism – many people thought Jack the Ripper must be Jewish as an 'Englishman' couldn't possibly have done it – pointing police to a suspect largely because he was Jewish.

Police did follow up media suggestions that 'Leather Apron' was the culprit, but this was proved to be a waste of time as he had solid alibis for the first two murders. Police also followed up other media suggestions that came to nothing.

Criticising the police was common in the media and led to mistrust, which may have hindered people coming forward with genuine and useful information.

It's less useful as it's just one account and there's no detail on how this report was received by police, or how much time they wasted following it up.

Source B: Useful because it's a description by a detective on the impact of the reward and the hundreds of mostly useless pieces of information which had to be read and some investigated. It's less useful because the detective may want to exaggerate its impact to try to direct blame for the lack of success in catching the murderer away from the police.

Own knowledge should confirm that the police were indeed inundated with information from the general public that took time to read and then investigate.

42. Practice

2 (b) Detail in Source B that I would follow up: 'Some of these cases we have sent men to investigate'.

Question I would ask: How many cases were investigated from this information supplied by the public?

What type of source I could use: Official records from H Division of the Met.

How this might help answer my question: It would give details of what investigations were done and on what basis.

43. Practice

3 Any one from:

- 18th century punishments were heavily based on retribution – punishing the person for what they'd done. In the 20th century, retribution is just one of the many aims of punishment.
- 18th century punishments were heavily based on deterrence – wanting to prevent others from committing the same crime by giving a harsh punishment. In the 20th century, deterrence is just one of the many aims of punishment.
- 20th century punishments aim at rehabilitating the criminal to some extent so they reform their lives and do not re-offend. Rehabilitation and reform were only just beginning to emerge as aims of punishment in the 18th century.
- 20th century punishments often aim at paying back society for what a criminal has done – hence the increase in community-based punishments. This was not a consideration in the 18th century.

44. Practice

4 Answer could include:

- Peel's ending of the Bloody Code in the 1820s, so there were far fewer capital crimes and punishment was more proportionate to the crime committed.
- An increase in alternative punishments, such as transportation and especially imprisonment, which were still seen as providing retribution to the criminal (but not unfairly so) while still acting as a deterrent to others and removing the criminal from society, so they could not re-offend.
- An increase in understanding of the reasons why people committed some crimes (e.g. theft for survival of yourself and/or your family) meant that it was seen as unfair to kill someone essentially just for being poor.
- A rise in the idea that punishment should be about reforming the criminal (as well as punishing them to act as a deterrent to others) – the death penalty left no opportunity for reform.

- Increasing awareness that the police and judicial system made mistakes – no way of rectifying this if a wrongly convicted person had already been hanged (highlighted through cases such as Timothy Evans, hanged for murder but it was later proved that he hadn't done it).
- Greater knowledge of the unfairness of the system through controversial cases, such as Derek Bentley (hanged even though he didn't actually kill and had severe learning difficulties) and Ruth Ellis (hanged even though she'd killed her violently abusive partner).
- Changes to the law so the death penalty for murder was suspended in 1965 and then abolished in 1969, and finally abolished for treason in 1999.

48. Practice

5 Answers must state how far the student agrees with the quotation. Evidence to support the statement includes:

- Forest Laws, which were new, impacted on a large number of people – about 30% of England became designated Royal Forest, so was subject to the new Forest Laws.
- Forest Laws were deeply resented, as were the foresters who enforced them, as they made illegal activities that were previously allowed and which many people had used for survival (e.g. food, fire wood and building materials).
- The other changes to crimes were mostly adjustments to existing laws (e.g. Murdrum fines – it was already a crime to murder someone and Wergild gave different punishments depending on the person killed) and the addition of Church courts were seen as a good as well as a bad thing (offering benefit of clergy so some men could get out of the death penalty, for example, and churches' punishments generally being more lenient that other courts).

Evidence against the statement includes:

- Murdrum fines essentially made it a worse crime to kill a Norman than any other person, which was pretty significant (although not a new change of direction) and applied to the whole country.
- Church courts arguably impacted on a greater number of people because they began to make judgements on moral actions, such as infidelity.

52. Practice

6 Answers must state how far the student agrees with the quotation. Evidence to support the statement includes:

- Communities expected to raise awareness of crime and chase and catch suspects through the hue and cry.
- Members of the community selected to join the sheriff's posse to catch suspects.
- Members of the community volunteered to join the night watch in some towns.
- Community nominated one of its members as the constable to lead the hue and cry and run the night watch.

Evidence against the statement includes:

- Some methods of community law enforcement had been abolished by this time – trial by ordeal and trial by combat.
- Justices of the Peace were appointed by the king (not the community) after the Justices of the Peace Act of 1361. JPs tried smaller crimes in local courts.
- Sheriffs were appointed by government. Their role included taking suspects for trial and was expanded to include tracking down criminals who hadn't been caught by the hue and cry. They were allowed to form a posse of local men to help with this task.

Published by Pearson Education Limited, 80 Strand, London, WC2R 0RL.

www.pearsonschoolsandfecolleges.co.uk

Copies of official specifications for all Pearson qualifications may be found on the website: qualifications.pearson.com

Text and illustrations © Pearson Education Limited 2017
Produced, typeset and illustrated by Tech-Set Ltd, Gateshead
Cover illustration by Eoin Coveney

The right of Kirsty Taylor to be identified as author of this work has been asserted by her in accordance with the Copyright, Designs and Patents Act 1988.

Content is included from Rob Bircher, Brian Dowse, and Victoria Payne.

First published 2017

20 19 18

10 9 8 7 6 5

British Library Cataloguing in Publication Data
A catalogue record for this book is available from the British Library

ISBN 978 1 292 16970 5

Copyright notice
All rights reserved. No part of this publication may be reproduced in any form or by any means (including photocopying or storing it in any medium by electronic means and whether or not transiently or incidentally to some other use of this publication) without the written permission of the copyright owner, except in accordance with the provisions of the Copyright, Designs and Patents Act 1988 or under the terms of a licence issued by the Copyright Licensing Agency, Barnard's Inn, 86 Fetter Lane, London EC4A 1EN (www.cla.co.uk). Applications for the copyright owner's written permission should be addressed to the publisher.

Printed in Slovakia by Neografia

Acknowledgements
The publisher would like to thank the following for their kind permission to reproduce their photographs:

(Key: b-bottom; c-centre; l-left; r-right; t-top)

akg-images Ltd: Liszt Collection 11tr; **Alamy Stock Photo:** Ashley Cooper Pics 21cl, Chronicle 11tl, 15, 17tr, Heritage Image Partnership Ltd 25tl, Ian Dagnall 4, John Frost Newspapers 29, Lebrecht Music & Arts Photo Library 10, Mark Boulton 6cr, Mary Evans Picture Library 14, 17cl, 17cr, Motoring Picture Library 20br, Pictorial Press Ltd 33, Reflex Picture Library 11cl, Trinity Mirror / Mirropix 24l, 24c, 24r, World History Archive 12; **Bridgeman Art Library Ltd:** Private Collection 18tl, 26; **British Library Images Online:** 6br; **Getty Images:** Hulton Archive 25br, Mark Douet 22, Past Pix 23, Peter Macdiarmid 19br; **Mary Evans Picture Library:** Bruce Castle Museum 13, Grenville Collins Postcard Collection 19tr, Metropolitan Police Authority 18bc; **Shutterstock.com:** Evgeny Murtola 21cr, SergeyIT 20tl; **TopFoto:** HIP 11cr

All other images © Pearson Education

Picture Research by: Alison Prior

Notes from the publisher

1.In order to ensure that this resource offers high-quality support for the associated Pearson qualification, it has been through a review process by the awarding body. This process confirms that this resource fully covers the teaching and learning content of the specification or part of a specification at which it is aimed. It also confirms that it demonstrates an appropriate balance between the development of subject skills, knowledge and understanding, in addition to preparation for assessment.

Endorsement does not cover any guidance on assessment activities or processes (e.g. practice questions or advice on how to answer assessment questions), included in the resource nor does it prescribe any particular approach to the teaching or delivery of a related course.

While the publishers have made every attempt to ensure that advice on the qualification and its assessment is accurate, the official specification and associated assessment guidance materials are the only authoritative source of information and should always be referred to for definitive guidance.

Pearson examiners have not contributed to any sections in this resource relevant to examination papers for which they have responsibility.

Examiners will not use endorsed resources as a source of material for any assessment set by Pearson.

Endorsement of a resource does not mean that the resource is required to achieve this Pearson qualification, nor does it mean that it is the only suitable material available to support the qualification, and any resource lists produced by the awarding body shall include this and other appropriate resources.

2.Pearson has robust editorial processes, including answer and fact checks, to ensure the accuracy of the content in this publication, and every effort is made to ensure this publication is free of errors. We are, however, only human, and occasionally errors do occur. Pearson is not liable for any misunderstandings that arise as a result of errors in this publication, but it is our priority to ensure that the content is accurate. If you spot an error, please do contact us at resourcescorrections@pearson.com so we can make sure it is corrected.